BOOMER BUILDINGS

Mid-Century Architecture Reborn

Mitchell | Giurgola
Architects

Published in Australia in 2005 by
The Images Publishing Group Pty Ltd
ABN 89 059 734 431
6 Bastow Place, Mulgrave, Victoria, 3170, Australia
Telephone: +61 3 9561 5544 Fax: +61 3 9561 4860
books@images.com.au
www.imagespublishing.com

ISBN 1 92074 496 7

Edited by Michael J. Crosbie, Ph.D., RA
Designed by You-Chang Jeon, Mitchell | Giurgola Architects, LLP, New York, New York

Production by The Graphic Image Studio Pty Ltd, Mulgrave, Australia
www.tgis.com.au

Printed by Everbest Printing Co. Ltd, in Hong Kong/China

IMAGES has included on its website a page for special notices in relation to this and our other
publications. Please visit: www.imagespublishing.com

CONTENTS

PREFACE

The genesis of this book occurred in 1997 when Steve Goldberg began to develop a proposal for a paper to be presented at the 33rd annual Society for College and University Planners Conference to be held in Vancouver. The conference theme was "Crossing Boundaries – Making Connections." It occurred to Steve that we had worked on many mid-century buildings, imbuing them with new life and reintegrating them into their surroundings. These newly renovated buildings "cross the boundary" from yesterday to today and establish a "connection" to their neighbors and users. The paper that resulted, entitled "1960's Buildings: Innovative Transformations for the 90's" was delivered at the 1998 AIA Convention in San Francisco and the 1999 SCUP National Convention in Atlanta. The responses we received to these presentations served to confirm our conviction that there was significant interest in the subject of transforming mid-century buildings, an ever-increasing phenomenon.

In early 2003 we met with Paul Latham, director of The Images Publishing Group, and Steve proposed the idea for a book that would present case studies of some of the key M | G projects that deal with mid-century building renovations and/or additions. We trust that *Boomer Buildings: Mid-Century Architecture Reborn* will add to the body of knowledge about these buildings and heighten the awareness of both the public and professionals as to their potential worth and transformational value.

Special thanks go to Steve for bringing the book to the table and giving direction to the project; to partners Jan, Paul, John, Jim and Carol for lending their strong support to the endeavor; and to the entire staff for their tireless commitment to bringing buildings back from brink of oblivion with art and efficiency. We offer a special tribute to architect You-Chang Jeon for his dedicated leadership in the design and graphic choreography of the book and its case studies.

The Partners

Mitchell | Giurgola Architects

FOREWORD

Boomer Buildings: Mid-Century Architecture Reborn
Mitchell | Giurgola Architects

A recent article in *The New York Times* reported on the escalating demise of buildings designed and constructed during the post-war years—the hard-edged, unforgiving, sterile, and humorless creations of modernism's aging gurus and their uninspired copyists. The article noted that the rush to crush these aging Brutalist monoliths is difficult to argue with. Even on their best days, these buildings were not easy to love. They had (and in many cases continue to have) substandard heating and air-conditioning systems, poor lighting, minimal chase space, drafty exterior walls, asbestos and other toxic materials, crumbling concrete exposing rusting rebar, not to mention urban rudeness, contextual hostility, and monumental invulnerability. If the Cuban Missile Crisis had ended badly in 1962, archeologists millennia hence would have had not much else to judge the culture by than these baby-boomer bunkers.

Today, "Boomer Buildings" are energy sieves and (for their owners) money pits. Ripping them down seems like the kindest thing to do (and poetic justice for the works of designers who themselves had little sympathy for historic structures). Mitchell | Giurgola Architects shows that there is a far more intelligent and creative answer than the wrecking ball.

The near-death of Boomer Buildings comes precisely at the point when sustainable design and construction have captured the architectural spotlight. It's as if a miracle cure has been found just as we are pulling the plug on Brutalism and its offspring. In an age of diminishing natural resources (including buildable lots) architects and their clients need to know about an environmentally sustainable alternative to new construction: new life for old buildings, especially Boomer Buildings.

This book presents six case-study Boomer Buildings (each more than a generation old) that were on the brink of oblivion. Mitchell | Giurgola Architects worked closely with the client to determine how each project could be salvaged by incorporating updated program elements to serve a new generation of users. All six case studies present in lavish detail how each project is analyzed, from its energy use and curtainwall performance to its mechanical, electrical, and plumbing systems, and structural stability. The buildings often expand in size, with a seamless melding of new and old. Contemporary curtainwalls not only improve building performance, but also lend a fresh aesthetic appeal. In some cases, the original building's urban enmity and contextual boorishness are tamed with new wings that create hospitable courtyards. The results are born-again buildings revived at a fraction of the cost of a new facility built from scratch, and at the expense of far fewer natural resources.

Today, our cities and suburbs are peppered with buildings of the same vintage as those profiled here that are on the brink of failure, and are excellent candidates for rebirth. Mitchell | Giurgola documents a new, more sustainable approach to design and construction that builds on the past, and makes the old better than the new.

Michael J. Crosbie, Ph.D.

Dr. Crosbie is an architect, teacher, journalist, and critic whose work has been published internationally.

INTRODUCTION

Buildings constructed in the United States during the 1950s, 60s, and 70s, at the peak of the post-World War II building boom—in the very heart of the "Baby Boomer" generation—met the housing, work place, and educational needs of the Baby Boomers and compensated for the dearth of construction during the Great Depression and the war years. The sheer magnitude of the nation's inventory of buildings from this period dramatically altered our cities, towns, suburbs, campuses, and industrial and commercial landscapes. Many of these buildings which we refer to in shorthand as "Boomer Buildings" were partially shaped by newly invented (but not thoroughly tested) building products and systems, which today are both physically and functionally obsolete. Because the decision to renovate and adaptively reuse can often be justified over the alternative to tear down and rebuild from scratch, such buildings, in the aggregate, are the profession's next great design and technological opportunity.

Nearly every college and university campus is facing the necessity to repair or replace significant buildings built during the Boomer years. Campuses will increasingly be called upon to adapt these functionally and technically obsolete buildings according to new approaches to education, with needs and technical requirements that are radically different than those of the original building. Several factors are driving the wholesale re-examination of Boomer-era construction on college and university campuses:

- · the failure of exterior materials, including entire curtainwalls, insulation, gaskets, and sealants;

- · substandard mechanical/electrical equipment and distribution systems are at the end of their useful lives;

- · new teaching delivery methods and pedagogics are requiring colleges and universities to examine the efficacy of their classroom stock;

- · infilled and expanded campus plans, which now isolate many Boomer Buildings within campus plans;

- · the desire to reintegrate these radically different structures into the physical and spatial fabric of the campus.

This book traces the evolution of six Boomer Buildings constructed between the 1950s and 1970s that were at the end of their useful life—on the brink of extinction—and were resuscitated for new life. Many of them are on college campuses. With the sheer quantity of building stock from this era, several lessons can be gleaned from Mitchell | Giurgola's work in this realm that are applicable to other educational institutions as well as other kinds of public and private clients.

General characteristics of Boomer Buildings

The construction that took place in the post-war Baby Boomer era marked the last gasp of the declining International Style. At least three basic esthetics were in conflict—those of Wright, Mies, and Le Corbusier. The often original and brilliant late works of these modern masters, as well as the outstanding architecture of the best of their immediate followers, never constituted a coherent post-war version of the International Style. With the publication of Robert Venturi's *Complexity and Contradiction in Architecture* in 1966, postmodernist theory and practice entered the intellectual life of architecture, but was not to reach full force and virtually eradicate all traces of the modern movement in the U.S. until the following two decades. In the field of general office and institutional construction, however, the Miesian version of the International Style did triumph. Unfortunately, many (if not most) of these buildings are debased, banal, and reductive versions of Mies' powerful esthetic—the functional and structural formulas that helped to shape the seminal works of modern architecture.

Nevertheless, there is much to be said for this architectural period. The modernist dictum that "form follows function" led architects to clearly reveal and strongly express programmatic components and structure. The contradictory Miesian mandate that buildings be pavilions of universal, flexible space was also successfully followed. Design of typical buildings of the era emphasized speed of construction, efficiency, and low cost.

Structural systems consisted of modular, concrete, or steel skeleton frames, typically with low floor-to-floor heights and little redundancy (a synopsis of pros and cons of Boomer Buildings is found on page 9).

Glass and metal or glass and precast concrete panel curtainwall facades were widely used to enclose almost every building type, and poured or precast concrete bearing walls were also specified, but far less frequently. All of these modular, repetitive systems used vast stretches of glass to bring light and views to interiors. But the glass was not designed to be energy efficient because energy in the post-war era was relatively inexpensive (up until the early 1970s).

Revising and expanding space for new functions

Boomer Buildings that are being brought back from the brink of extinction all have new programs or programmatic requirements. The functions that these structures originally housed have changed, or their requirements are different, calling for wholesale internal and external modifications and expansions. The internal redesigns often include more amenities and communal facilities for the occupants than those of the original structure. It is often necessary to relocate or add corridors, elevators, and stairs to meet current codes and functional needs.

Today's more sophisticated and space-demanding mechanical/electrical/plumbing and telecommunication systems require the creation of new, or the adaptation of existing, cubic feet that can be devoted to electric and telecommunications closets and vertical shafts. The new uses for these buildings often require a greater number of occupants, and such expanded building populations must be met with expanded recreational, dining, and toilet facilities. Such a reconfiguration of circulation and MEP support space can be conveniently handled within the modular steel-frame skeleton frameworks of most Boomer Buildings, with their easily penetrated or removable metal decks, and non-bearing interior walls.

In designing exterior additions and extensions, Mitchell | Giurgola has tried to ameliorate what we consider to be a negative contextual aspect of the architecture of this period—the fact that so many structures were designed as self-referential "object buildings" generally unrelated to the neighboring context, street, site, climate, and vernacular architecture. The new additions and facades are designed in such a way as to create new linkages between the building and its immediate environment.

Reversing curtainwall and functional obsolescence

The exterior enclosure systems of most of the Boomer Buildings that Mitchell | Giurgola has worked on have reached the end of their useful lives because they do not meet today's functional needs, codes, standards, and requirements. Those of prefabricated metal and glass had unexpectedly short life spans, and began to fall apart after little more than one generation of use. The window glass has become discolored, the sash corroded and not weather-tight, the metal panels stained. The simplicity and inefficiency of these walls produced higher solar infiltration and thermal transmission loads that resulted in greater heating and cooling requirements and much higher energy costs.

Because these aging enclosure systems are in such decrepit condition, generally such walls do not merit the expense of restoration. Instead, they are often replaced with the more energy-efficient systems available today. A complete facade replacement offers the opportunity to give the building a more contemporary image that may also better respond to context, reflect new programs, and (if necessary) ameliorate site-related acoustic problems. Fortunately, because these non-bearing skins are easy to remove, they are excellent candidates for replacement.

Accommodating today's mechanical and electrical equipment

Transforming Boomer Buildings requires removal or conversion of outdated, energy-inefficient, oversized mechanical equipment and controls. Still viable systems, such as many of the robust built-up air-handling units, can be refitted with energy-conserving variable-speed fan drives and modern digital controls that allow reduced energy use when space loads are at less than peak levels. Equipment that has reached the end of its useful life (such as chillers) can be replaced with substantially more efficient, CFC-free modern versions. The existing infrastructure of piping distribution can often be reused, if it has been well maintained. Electrical systems must often be substantially replaced or upgraded because electrical code requirements and usage patterns by occupants have changed. At the same time, life safety and fire management systems have dramatically changed in response to fast-evolving technology, hard-earned knowledge, and enhanced codes. The completely new infrastructure and distribution requirements of today's communications, video, and data technology must be designed and installed in a cost-effective way that anticipates continuing future changes in technology.

While major equipment, lights, and computer equipment have become much more energy conservative, air conditioning and power demands have not dropped correspondingly. Recent trends, in response to rising costs and greater competition, have resulted in greater occupancy levels per floor. More people per floor means more computers, servers, scanners, printers, telephones, and fax machines, as well as higher cooling loads per floor. More equipment requires more wiring and receptacles, as well as increased telecommunications distribution and infrastructure. At the same time, there is increasing demand that all systems be substantially more reliable and available on a 24/7 basis.

Typical impact of boomer buildings

The City University of New York (CUNY) provides a broad overview of the issues involved in resuscitating Boomer Buildings, and their potential impact on a client's resources. The country's largest public university has 20 campuses comprising 11 four-year colleges, six two-year colleges, and three graduate schools. CUNY's entire physical plant comprises 275 buildings, totals 23.5 million square feet, and is located throughout New York City's five boroughs.

CUNY's total building stock started to increase significantly during the 1950s and continued to rise steadily during the next three decades. The buildings of the 1960s and 1970s are distinguished from buildings of earlier decades by differences that are more acute and with consequences that are magnified in proportion to the large quantity of those buildings. During these two decades, CUNY added 36.3 percent of the university's current total building inventory.

For more than a decade, extending the life and usefulness of Boomer Buildings has consumed a large part of CUNY's capital improvement program. While many of these renovation efforts have been very successful, in other instances careful evaluations have prompted CUNY to demolish aging Boomers. Many of the criteria considered in these evaluations are technical and quantifiable. But other values that now guide CUNY planners are more intangible, having less to do with functional considerations and more with issues of context and appropriateness.

Boomer Buildings represent a significant cultural shift in campus design, noticeable in elements ranging from siting and scale to construction methods and materials. The buildings appear as deliberate renunciations of prior norms, of familiar patterns, of their surroundings, and ultimately of familiarity itself. Set apart by a new vocabulary of forms, these new buildings were physically apart from the campus order that governed their neighbors. Although even good ideas can be realized poorly and no epoch is immune to shoddiness, the departures of Boomer Buildings seem to have made them particularly vulnerable to problematic realizations.

During this period, the break with current conventions was motivated by a drive for construction economy, efficient space utilization, and the benefits of new (often untested) technologies. While windows grew larger to bring more light and air to spaces, almost everything else grew smaller: wall and floor dimensions, and the amount of space available for equipment, support functions, and communal uses. While floor plans became more generic and thus flexible, many architectural elements (such as those needed to communicate a hierarchy of uses and places) virtually vanished.

In some cases, these buildings were so architecturally impoverished that they turned into maintenance and functional problems upon completion, and are entirely untenable 30 years later. The most striking examples of these problems are characterized by anti-contextual architectural siting and expression, along with poor construction.

CUNY's planners are now trying to blunt the divisive results of the rebellion of earlier generations of architects and builders and seek an enriching coexistence. Echoing a national pattern where older public structures, neglected since the Boomer years, are being revitalized, one of the highest values guiding CUNY's capital program is the affirmation of the campus as a family of structures, not a collection of unrelated facilities. This approach is clearly seen in Mitchell | Giurgola's revitalization of Powdermaker Hall on CUNY's Queens College campus (see page 32) as well as in our master plan for that campus.

The future of Boomer Buildings

Through Mitchell | Giurgola's experience in renovating Boomer Buildings, we have learned that the functional and physical obsolescence of exterior walls, MEP systems, telecommunications systems, and asbestos generally

requires wholesale changes as opposed to minor corrections, restoration, or phased construction. On the other hand, for all their esthetic and functional faults, the straightforward modular, industrial nature of Boomer Buildings has facilitated successful adaptations to context and programmatic change. In remodeling these buildings we have created opportunities to improve their relationship to sites and general surroundings. We have discovered the strengths and weaknesses of the building products and systems introduced during the Baby Boomer generation. We are utilizing those that have stood the test of time as well as the many improved materials and technologies available today.

Boomer Buildings Pros and Cons

Pros	Cons
· Flexibility	· Impermanence
· Rational grid/modularity	· Low floor-to-floor heights
· Emphasis on light and air	· Lack of communal spaces/lobbies
· Minimalism/efficiency	· No redundancy
· Clear orientation	· End of useful life of systems
· Rational, understandable	· Energy inefficiency
· Experimentation with new materials	· Anti-contextual
· New curtainwall systems	· Failure of new materials
· Celebration of structure	· Wholesale replacement of skin required
· Easily re-adapted	· Lack of accessibility of systems
	· Substandard code compliance (ADA, fire, life safety)

Total Renovation/New Skins

- The Lighthouse International Headquarters

- Powdermaker Hall Renovation

- New York County Family Court
  Building Renovation

1991
Concept Design

Schematic Design

Design Development
1992
Construction
Document

Construction
1993

1994

Completion

1995

1996

1997

1998

1999

2000

2001

2002

2003

2004

2005

2006

THE LIGHTHOUSE INTERNATIONAL HEADQUARTERS

New York, New York

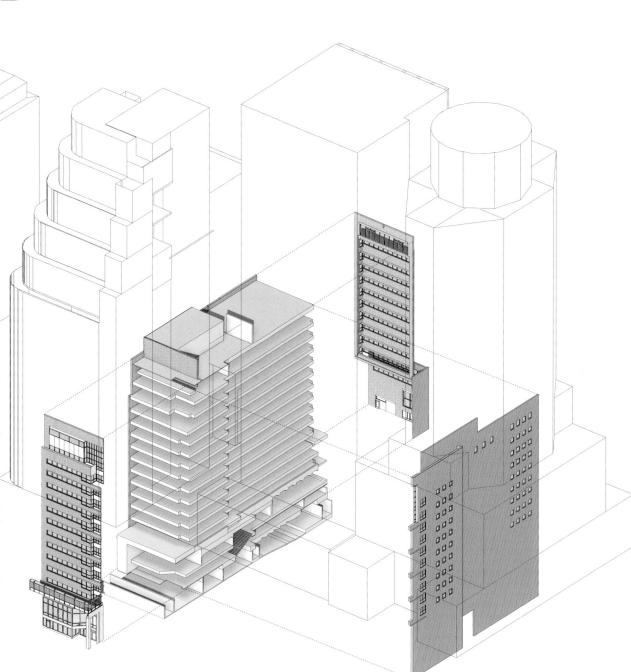

- New Program
- Updated Program
- Updated Circulation
- New MEP Telecom System
- Asbestos Removal
- New Exterior Wall
- Addition
- Renovation

The existing Manhattan Lighthouse Headquarters facility consisted of a 14-story office tower on East 59th Street, completed in 1964, connected to a six-story 50's building facing 60th Street. These two buildings no longer served the needs of a newly expanded program that called for a multi-facility building that includes a street-level store, a performing arts and conference center, a child development center, a low-vision clinic, computer technology and employment training facilities, a music school and library, vision and research labs, and administrative and office space.

This program required the complete rehabilitation of the institution's existing quarters. After evaluating the existing facility, it was determined that because of greatly increased use, an obsolete HVAC system and new HVAC requirements, and the need to remove asbestos and expand elevator capacity, the 60th Street building should be replaced with a single 16-story tower. The structural frame of the 1964 building was reused with a floor added to the basement and the top. It is attached to a 16-story addition constructed on the site of the completely demolished 60th Street building. The first floors of the existing 59th Street tower extend to the property line, filling the former 16-foot-deep plaza once required by zoning regulations.

Area: 170,000 gross square feet
85,500 square foot addition
84,500 square foot renovation

Context and Site

The Lighthouse Headquarters occupies a through-block site on 59th Street between Park and Lexington Avenues in the heart of East Midtown Manhattan. It is located between Bloomingdale's to the east and FAO Schwartz to the west, along a stretch of highly active retail and commercial office development. The 1960's building it occupied on the 59th Street side of the site was set back from the facades of its adjacent neighbors and created a break in what was otherwise a continuous, ground-level retail experience.

The 60th Street side of the site contained a 6-story 1950's structure, which is flanked by town houses to the west and a town house and multi-story apartment building to the east. East 60th Street marks the transition from commercial office development to the south and residential development to the north. The narrow through-block footprint of the site presented a significant challenge in providing daylight to the interior of the building.

Since the completion of the 1960's building, The Lighthouse experienced a qualitative and quantitative change in its programs, which required both a new image and additional space. To gain that space, the 60th Street building, which could not support additional floors, was demolished and replaced by a new 16-story addition linked floor-by-floor to the 59th Street building, to which was added a floor at the basement and top. The qualitative change in the building was marked by the creation of a new, highly public conference/performing arts center at the base of the building extending to the property line on 59th Street, new vertical transportation and MEP systems, and a new exterior skin.

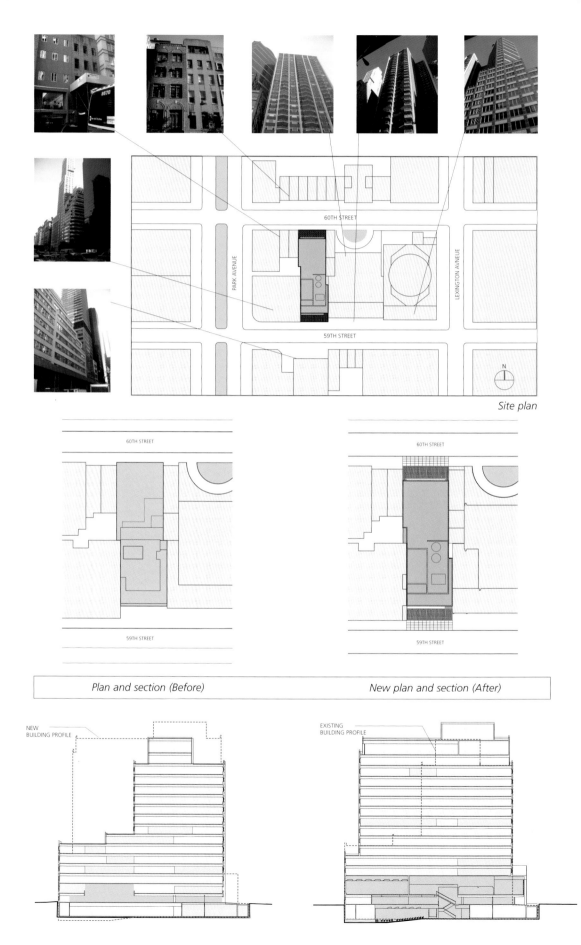

Site plan

Plan and section (Before)   New plan and section (After)

■ Public space
□ Shared space

The inclusion of the conference/performing arts center at the base of the building resulted in a significant transformation of the existing program. The existing flat-floor multipurpose room was replaced with a new sloped-floor theater/auditorium at the lower level and a multipurpose room on the second floor, both of which were linked by a newly created three-story open staircase. This freed up the ground level for an expanded lobby on 59th Street, conference rooms, and the Child Development Center bus arrival and pick-up area on 60th Street. The cafeteria, hidden away on the fourth floor, was moved to the second floor along with a new kitchen, giving it a strong visual connection to activity on 59th Street as well as a physical one to the multipurpose room and open staircase. The Child Development Center, located on the sixth floor, was relocated to the third floor so it could utilize the roof of the newly extended base on 59th Street as a south-facing outdoor play area. The elevators, previously located inconveniently off the main circulation corridor were moved to the west in their own separate alcove, away from the main circulation paths.

The tower portion of the 1960's building was stripped to its structural frame. Program elements that experienced the highest traffic were located on the lower levels. The core of the building, containing toilets, fire stairs, and electrical/data closets was relocated to the west side, along with the elevators. The existing single source building-wide air conditioning system was replaced with fan rooms on each floor to serve the different operating schedules of each floor's various program components, providing around-the-clock availability without running the whole building. The precast concrete facade, with energy inefficient single pane windows, was replaced with insulated glass ribbon windows to maximize daylighting in the offices and classrooms. The failing windowless east facade party wall was removed and replaced with a wall with punched openings to provide needed daylight into the middle zones of the long narrow through-block floor plate.

View in 1970

Axonometric diagram (Before)

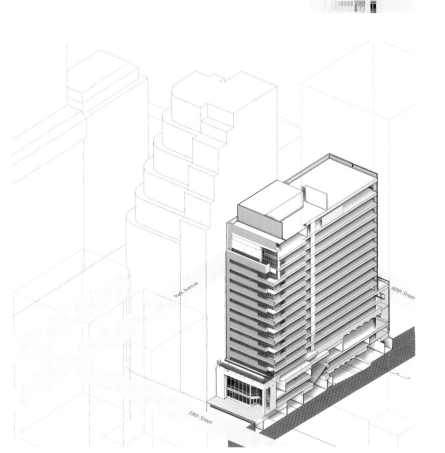

Axonometric diagram (After)

The Lighthouse wanted the addition and renovation to reflect its new mission of assisting its visually impaired clientele to function effectively in mainstream society. It also wanted the building to be a model of accessibility and universal design. The need to demolish the 1950's building and replace the energy inefficient windows, and the failing party wall of the 1960's building, presented a unique opportunity to create a new and unified image for The Lighthouse.

Alternative design studies were prepared orienting the main entry of the conference/performing arts center on 59th and 60th Streets. Ultimately, The Lighthouse chose the former approach, where it had maintained its presence since the early 1900s. In both solutions, the new building was intended to act as a "beacon" to its occupants by allowing its programs to emanate through a newly vitalized base, ribbon windows above, and a special top which radiated light, the stimulus source for vision.

   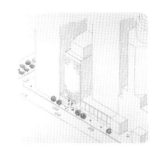 

The Lighthouse International Headquarters

The newly designed Lighthouse transformed the 1960's vertical monolith into a building with a base, middle, and top. The base continues the "street wall" of its neighbors, knitting the Lighthouse into the urban fabric. The middle is made more transparent through the use of ribbon windows, floor-to-ceiling glazing at the prominent northeast corner, and new punched windows in the party wall. The corner "Light Room" at the top contains an uplit ceiling with bands of the primary colors of light (red, blue, green), which when blended together form white light, which is normal to our vision. In the evening, the building radiates its inner light and becomes a beacon to the public.

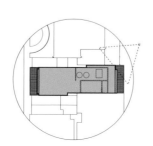

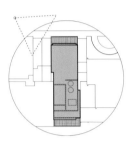

(Before)

View from Park Avenue to 60th Street

Elevation (60th Street)

In contrast to its predecessor's facade, which was recessive and anonymous, the 59th Street elevation responds to the variegated commercial and retail character of its neighbors by establishing a strong architectural presence through the grandly scaled treatment of its prominent northeast corner and new double-height entry portico. The roof of the portico serves as an outdoor play area for the Child Development Center. The tower is clad in a warm peach/rose colored masonry to reinforce its more open and welcoming image.

The 60th Street elevation relates to the adjacent town houses by means of a setback at the fifth floor. An additional setback was required by zoning at the fifteenth floor. In both cases the roof areas are used as terraces, which open to the lower-scaled residential area to the north.

| *Elevation (59th Street)* | *View from Park Avenue to 59th Street* | *(Before)* |

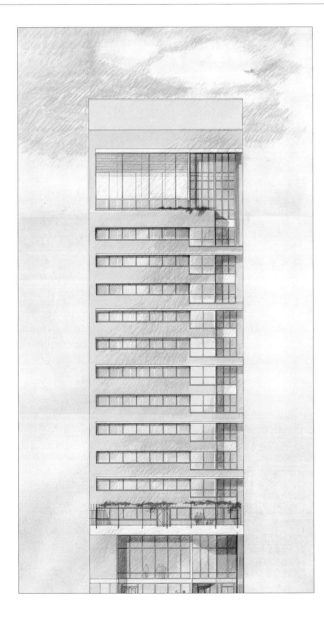

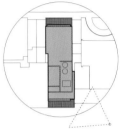

Entrance (Before)

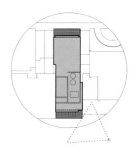

Entrance (After)

The newly created limestone entry portico frames the entry, a new Lighthouse store, and the cafeteria above. In contrast to its predecessor's dark, opaque and recessive presence, the new Lighthouse is luminous, transparent and welcoming, reflecting its new mainstreaming mission.

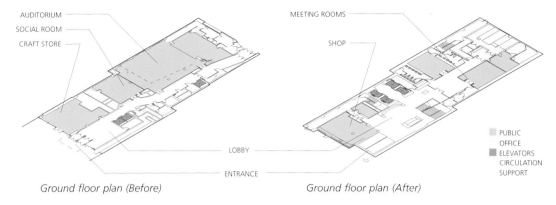

AUDITORIUM
SOCIAL ROOM
CRAFT STORE
LOBBY
ENTRANCE

MEETING ROOMS
SHOP

PUBLIC
OFFICE
ELEVATORS
CIRCULATION
SUPPORT

Ground floor plan (Before)

Ground floor plan (After)

Entrance – front view

In contrast to the casual layout of its predecessor, the renovated lobby is designed to provide clear paths of travel to the reception desk, performing arts center and programs in the tower. A clear sense of orientation is provided through the creation of a three-story atrium with a staircase connecting all levels of the performing arts center. Facilities in the tower portion of the building are accessed by elevators located in an alcove at a right angle to the staircase. Seating areas containing concave maple benches are also located in alcoves out of the paths of travel.

Stairs (Before)

Lobby stairs (After)

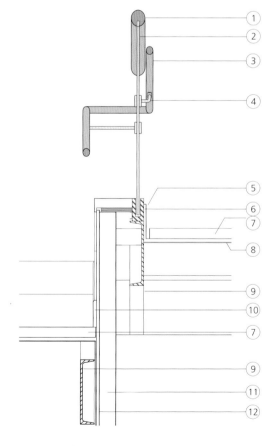

1	3" WOOD TOP RAIL	7	PRECAST TERRAZZO TREAD
2	TEMPERED GLASS		W/ ABRASIVE STRIP
3	1 1/2" WOOD HANDRAIL	8	METAL PAN
4	STAINLESS STEEL BRACKET	9	STEEL STRINGER
5	STEEL STRINGER	10	PRECAST TERRAZZO BASE
6	ALUMINUM SHOE	11	METAL STUD
		12	GYPSUM WALL BOARD

Entrance lobby – View 2

Entrance lobby (Before)

Lobby stairs – View 1

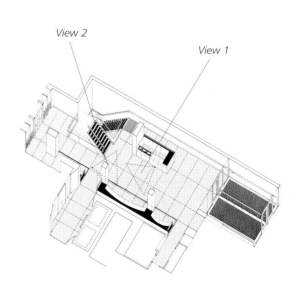

View 2

View 1

The cafeteria and boardroom in the old Lighthouse were sandwiched into its cellular structure, and were only distinguished from adjacent office and classroom areas by their furnishings. The double-height, flat-floor multipurpose room functioned best as a gym or large meeting room, but was marginal as an auditorium because of its poor sight lines. Additionally, its lighting was fixed and could not respond to changing venues. The rooms were drab and uninspired.

The new special rooms in The Lighthouse Headquarters were given a prominent location, form and lighting appropriate to their function. The cafeteria, multipurpose room and boardroom all benefit from controlled natural light and a visual connection to the life of the city. The light, both natural and electrical, is complementary and changing, establishing a powerful presence in each room, and creating a "house of light".

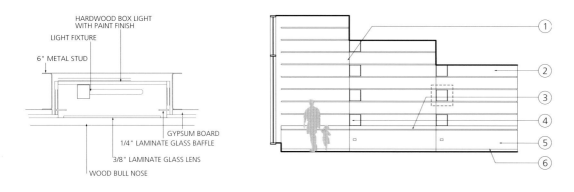

1 GYPSUM WALL CONTROL JOINT TO ALIGN W/ DROPPED SOFFIT ABOVE
2 PAINTED GYPSUM WALL BOARD
3 LUMBER CHAIR RAIL
4 CAFETERIA WALL LIGHT FIXTURE
5 VINYL WALL COVERING
6 WOOD BASE

Dining room

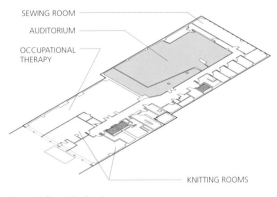
SEWING ROOM
AUDITORIUM
OCCUPATIONAL THERAPY
KNITTING ROOMS

Second floor (Before)

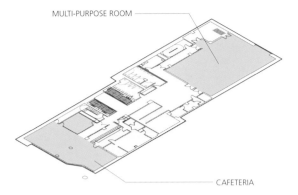
MULTI-PURPOSE ROOM
CAFETERIA

Second floor (After)

1 LINEAR DIFFUSER
2 SLATTED WOOD PANEL
3 VINYL WALLCOVERING
4 WALL CONTROL JOINT
5 LUMBER CHAIR RAIL

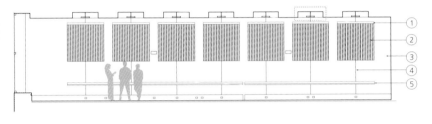

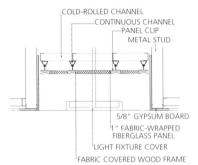
COLD-ROLLED CHANNEL
CONTINUOUS CHANNEL
PANEL CLIP
METAL STUD
5/8" GYPSUM BOARD
1" FABRIC-WRAPPED FIBERGLASS PANEL
LIGHT FIXTURE COVER
FABRIC COVERED WOOD FRAME

Multi-purpose room

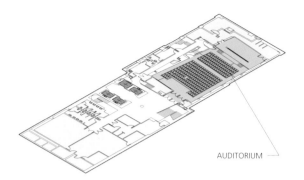

AUDITORIUM

Basement floor (After)

Auditorium (Before)

Auditorium

1 JOINTS IN WOOD PANELS
2 ACCESSIBLE WOOD SCREEN
   PANELS AT ORGAN PIPES
3 REVEAL
4 LIGHT PIPE BELOW DUCT

5 BAFFLE OF ACOUSTICALLY TRANSPARENT
   FABRIC WRAPPED FRAME AROUND DUCTS
6 BOTTOM OF DUCT OVER STAGE
   PROJECTION SCREEN

7 WOOD PIVOTING PANEL
8 DOOR TO BACKSTAGE IN
   PIVOTING PANEL / WALL
9 HARDWOOD BASE

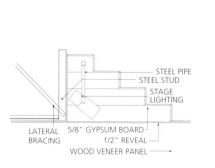

STEEL PIPE
STEEL STUD
STAGE
LIGHTING

LATERAL
BRACING

5/8" GYPSUM BOARD
1/2" REVEAL
WOOD VENEER PANEL

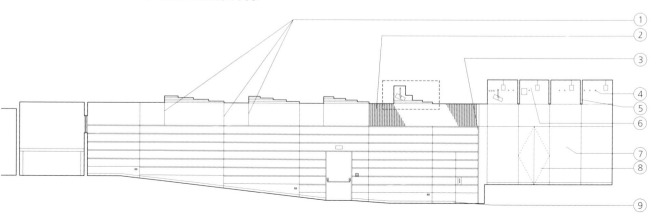

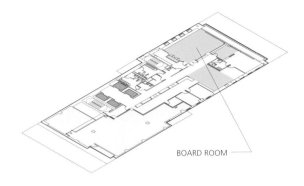

BOARD ROOM

Fifteenth floor (After)

Boardroom

1	WINDOW COVE	4	LEATHER BANQUETTE
2	BLACK-OUT SHADE COVE	5	SLAT WOOD GRILLE
3	LINEAR DIFFUSER	6	MAPLE BASE

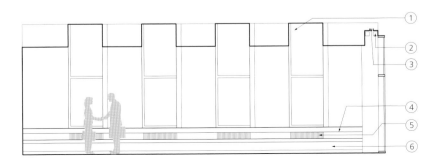

Given the need for a total overhaul of its obsolete MEP and transportation systems, removal of asbestos, and the construction of a new addition, it was decided to vacate the building entirely, rather than upgrade it on an incremental basis. The reuse of the existing structural steel frame of the 1964 building resulted in an approximate 10 percent reduction in overall construction cost.

Construction 59th Street

Construction 60th Street

1991

1992

1993

1994

1995

1996

Concept Design

1997

Schematic Design
Design Development
1998

1999

Construction
Document

2000
Construction

2001

2002

2003

Completion

2004

2005

2006

The 73-acre Queens College Campus is composed of 35 buildings constructed between the 1930s and the present. The campus layout was organized around a central green with buildings flanking three sides and open on the fourth with views of the Manhattan skyline. The campus started as a reform school for boys, with six stucco Spanish Revival barrel-tile-roofed buildings. The City University of New York (CUNY) acquired the campus in 1937 and new buildings gradually diffused the strength of the campus plan. Ad hoc development jeopardized the integrity and the efficient capacity of the campus for the long term.

In 1997 a master plan was developed by Mitchell | Giurgola as a comprehensive vision for the future of the college. Mitchell | Giurgola evaluated the programmatic needs of the institution, as well as the condition of the existing buildings, landscape, and infrastructure. Shifting academic emphases, growing computer needs, changes in teaching style, the aging of the existing building, and community issues all contributed to the need for a wholesale appraisal of the campus.

Site utilization patterns and distressed areas were documented. Also assessed were potential sites for new construction, buildings destined for demolition, buildings needing refurbishment, and landscaping and open spaces. An implementation or phasing plan delineated how to best serve and enhance the academic community.

As a first step in the implementation of the plan, Mitchell | Giurgola redesigned Powdermaker Hall—the largest classroom and faculty office structure on campus. Between the 1950s and 1997, no design guidelines had been established, and the haphazard appearance of the campus was the result. The upgrade of one of the most significant buildings on the main quadrangle allowed an opportunity to design facades that would mediate the diverse architectural styles of the surrounding buildings and set design guidelines for future construction. The commission to renovate Powdermaker (retaining only its structural frame) simultaneously with our preparation of the campus master plan was serendipitous but timely.

POWDERMAKER HALL RENOVATION
Queens College – The City University of New York

Flushing, New York

☐ New Program
■ Updated Program
■ Updated Circulation
■ New MEP Telecom System
☐ Asbestos Removal
■ New Exterior Wall
☐ Addition
■ Renovation

A. View from east

B. View from quadrangle

C. View of the quadrangle from the west

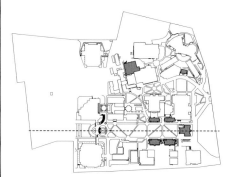

The campus in 1937 when CUNY acquired the site.

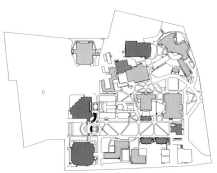

The campus in 1990 upon completion of two major growth periods.

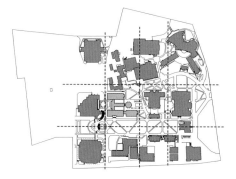

Major formal gestures to give an order to future development.

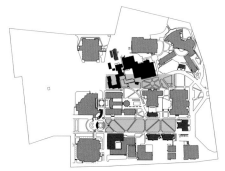

Long term plan for the forseeable future Building reprogramming, consolidations, and refurbishment will claim most available capital.

D. View of old Powdermaker Hall

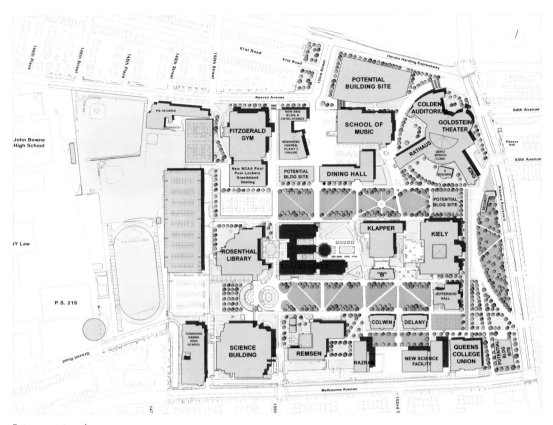

Future master plan

Campus view – 1920s

Existing campus plan

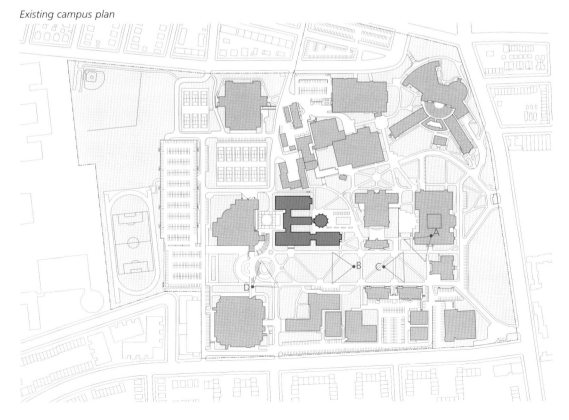

The challenge to CUNY is to focus on a series of modernizations and programmatic adjustments to repair a worn out campus that has suffered, as have campuses around the country, from insufficient maintenance, no modernization to speak of, and a physical plant that is unable to meet the challenges presented by the needs of the 21st century.

To provide a road map and set of guidelines for the future, the planning team has carried out a traditional assessment and analysis of the campus. Rather than projecting a campus as the site for major new development, the master plan amendment establishes a vision of a campus with good bones whose buildings need modernization; whose central utilities require upgrading; whose landscaping, site lighting, and vehicular and pedestrian circulation need improvement. These initiatives, while relatively "innocent" in isolation, in the aggregate create a new campus that reflects the vitality of the academic mission and will promote and enhance that mission.

Space utilization and the appropriateness of the various spaces to their function were evaluated. Calibrating the projected enrollment trends with the current building stock led to an interactive matrix that merges the quantity of space needed with the quality of space required to carry out the academic mission. What becomes apparent is that in many cases the amount of available space and its quality is not appropriate for the current occupants, but could well serve other users. The plan offers a combination of building upgrades and relocations that can be adjusted to CUNY funding cycles.

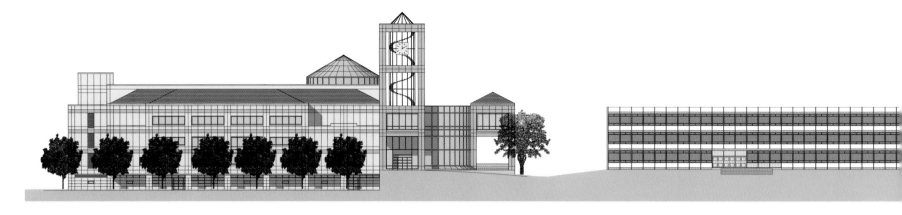

Rosenthal Library 1980s

Powdermaker Hall 1950s

Structure

The building's greatest asset lay in the concrete slabs and columns. While the floor-to-floor height is minimal at 11'4", the floor plate is very generous.

MEP

The MEP system consisted of perimeter fin-tube radiators, forced-air ventilation, and air-conditioning window units.

Exterior Wall

The exterior wall was glazed brick veneer over concrete block, and a finished window and curtainwall system that borrowed heavily from the Miesian tradition.

Exterior Wall

Because the building is in the path of LaGuardia Airport runways, single glazed, often open windows created havoc on classroom noise levels.

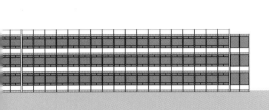
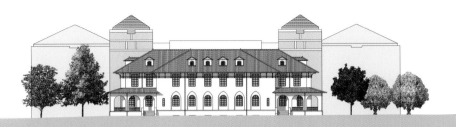

Powdermaker Hall Elevation (Before)

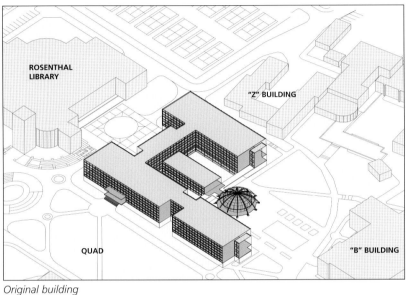

ROSENTHAL LIBRARY

"Z" BUILDING

QUAD

"B" BUILDING

Original building

Between the mid-1950s and 1997 no common ground was established for the design of new buildings or their siting. Mitchell | Giurgola's commission to re-design Powdermaker Hall simultaneously with the master plan provided the impetus to develop design guidelines for the preservation of campus open spaces, massing of new buildings, and design of building exteriors.

"B" Building 1920s

Entrance

Entrances were unattractive, with deteriorating, hazardous steps and no access for the disabled.

Service

No service provisions in the original building left an unmanageable refuse mess alongside the curb.

Interior

Interior corridors, while graciously wide, were poorly lit, had no views to the outside, and offered no amenities for students.

Stair

With no interior public spaces in the building, the 5-10,000 students and hundreds of faculty who use Powdermaker had no place to gather.

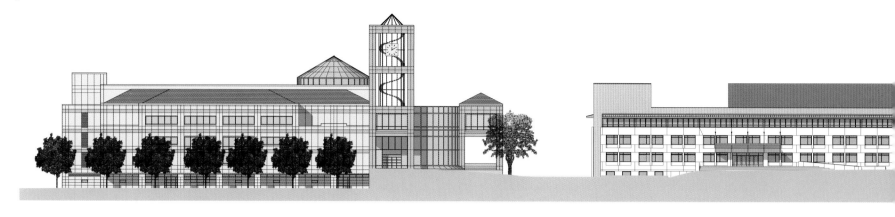

Powdermaker Hall Elevation (After)

The failure of the exterior envelope led the design team to recommend stripping it off to the building structure to allow for a new skin, which would be well-insulated from aircraft noise and temperature fluctuations; would maximize natural light while minimizing heat gain; and would mediate between buildings built in completely different styles to bring visual order to the campus. The addition of a mechanical system with necessary rooftop equipment also raised issues of changes to building massing.

As illustrated above, the solution revolves around the introduction of a soft, hand-molded red brick background cladding with applied precast concrete panels to relate to the modest scale of the stucco buildings from the 1930s. A continuous "strip" window with a protective "eyebrow" tied the building together and added a sloped element to relate to the adjacent Mission Style barrel-tile roofs. Red brick and off-white precast panels create a modulated facade that correlates with both the large scale of the Rosenthal Library and the intimacy of the stucco building on its opposite flank.

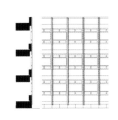

1 In his "domino" house of 1923, Le Corbusier codified the flexible essence of post-and-slab construction that became one of the primary tools of modern architecture. Mies van der Rohe brought a universally applicable cladding to this flexible construction. The combination created some wonderful, but similarly abstract architectural solutions to different programmatic concerns, such as the university buildings at IIT in Chicago and the Seagram Building in New York.

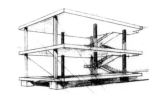

2 The plan organization of Powdermaker Hall also followed the tenets of modernist flexibility and its legacy proved to be particularly valuable in the adaptive reuse of the structure. The relatively thin, long bars of each wing of the building were easily adapted to classrooms large and small and a variety of office suites for all 11 departments that occupy the building.

3 The meager floor-to-floor height of 11' 4" (resulting from the desire for a highly efficient ratio of exterior wall to floor area) created enormous problems for the introduction of an HVAC system in the building that previously had relied upon natural ventilation.

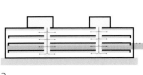
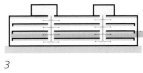

4 The outcome of the aforementioned issues led to a facade related to very specific environmental and contextual circumstances—characteristics quite different than those of the original architecture.

View of the longest facade, facing the historic quadrangle to the south. The cut at approximately the middle of the building serves to modulate the long facade and creates an outlook onto the campus from the central, interior corridor. This view describes well the balance between hand-set masonry and precast panels.

With respect to larger campus issues, Powdermaker Hall "steps back" to give full view of the library campanile, while the entry canopy projects outward to draw people to it.

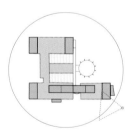

1 The design principle to modulate the overall massing of the 188,000 square structure utilizes two exterior cladding materials to articulate different elements of the enclosure. The overall volume, with its three long wings joined at one end, is clad in a "soft" hand-molded, sand-faced brick to ground the building, quite literally, with its earthy character. The penthouses are downplayed by grafting them onto this brick foundation.

2 Precast panels also highlight particular building elements such as the east entry. Two planes of precast walls slide past each other with transparent connections—symbols of porosity and accessibility.

3 Overlaid on the brick are precast concrete panels that define the occupied spaces, establish a scale related to passersby, and create with the brick the duality of earth tones and lightness of off-white. To "marry" these two materials a reveal between allows the precast to "float" off the brick background. Precast panels hang from the existing concrete floor slabs.

4 Aluminum windows are set into the precast panel system. In fact, they were designed to fit into the panels at the factory to reduce the amount of fieldwork; however, the contractor opted to install the windows on site. Every room has an operable sash for natural ventilation, if desired. Along the top floor a continuous strip window indicates the smaller module of office spaces inside and creates a "top" to the applied window/precast system.

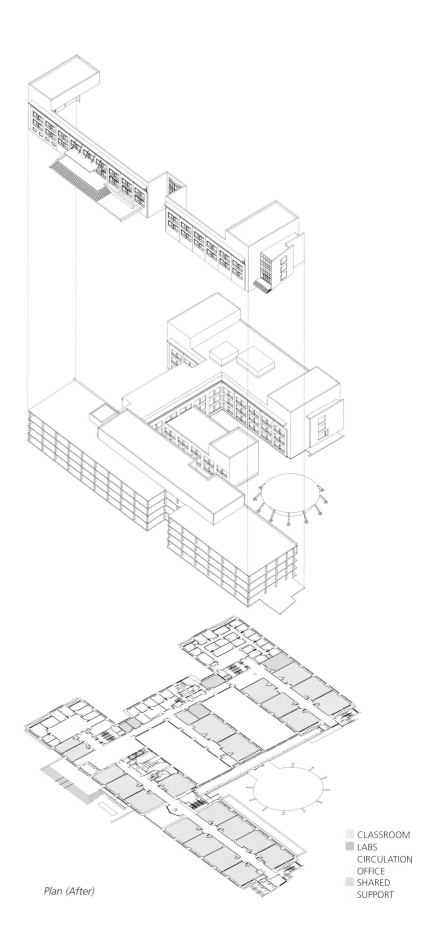

Plan (After)

CLASSROOM
LABS
CIRCULATION
OFFICE
SHARED
SUPPORT

Before

The plan illustrates the organization of the building with classroom floors dominating the first and second floors. The upper and lower floors house departmental office suites. Building services cluster near the ends of the wings, near stairs and shafts that will not restrict the potential for future reprogramming of space utilization.

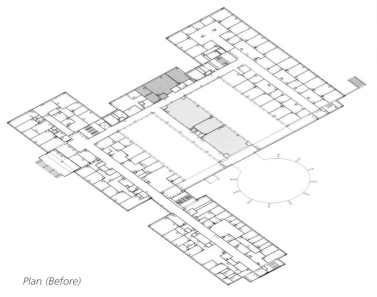

Plan (Before)

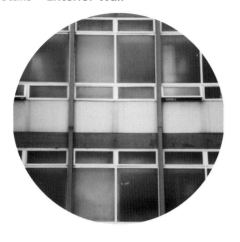

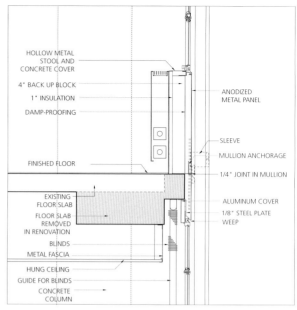

HOLLOW METAL STOOL AND CONCRETE COVER
4" BACK UP BLOCK
1" INSULATION
DAMP-PROOFING
ANODIZED METAL PANEL
SLEEVE
MULLION ANCHORAGE
FINISHED FLOOR
1/4" JOINT IN MULLION
EXISTING FLOOR SLAB
FLOOR SLAB REMOVED IN RENOVATION
ALUMINUM COVER
1/8" STEEL PLATE
WEEP
BLINDS
METAL FASCIA
HUNG CEILING
GUIDE FOR BLINDS
CONCRETE COLUMN

Typical section and elevation (Before)

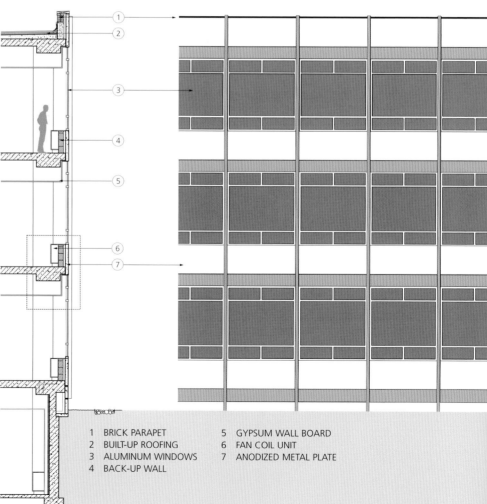

1 BRICK PARAPET	5 GYPSUM WALL BOARD
2 BUILT-UP ROOFING	6 FAN COIL UNIT
3 ALUMINUM WINDOWS	7 ANODIZED METAL PLATE
4 BACK-UP WALL	

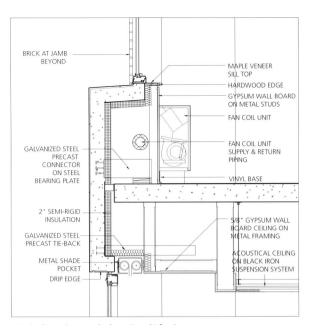

Typical section and elevation (After)

BRICK AT JAMB BEYOND

MAPLE VENEER SILL TOP
HARDWOOD EDGE
GYPSUM WALL BOARD ON METAL STUDS
FAN COIL UNIT

GALVANIZED STEEL PRECAST CONNECTOR ON STEEL BEARING PLATE

FAN COIL UNIT SUPPLY & RETURN PIPING

VINYL BASE

2" SEMI-RIGID INSULATION

5/8" GYPSUM WALL BOARD CEILING ON METAL FRAMING

GALVANIZED STEEL PRECAST TIE-BACK

ACOUSTICAL CEILING ON BLACK IRON SUSPENSION SYSTEM

METAL SHADE POCKET

DRIP EDGE

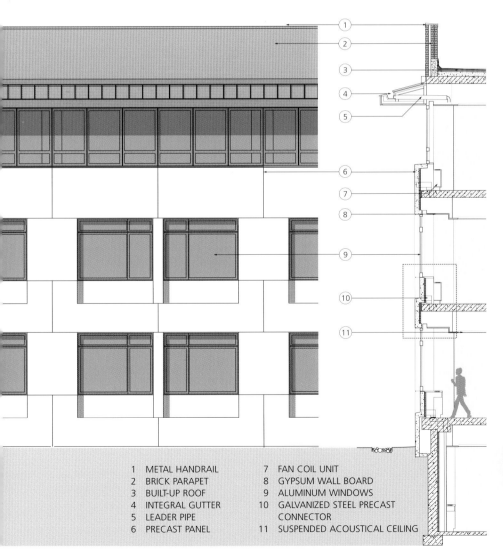

1. METAL HANDRAIL
2. BRICK PARAPET
3. BUILT-UP ROOF
4. INTEGRAL GUTTER
5. LEADER PIPE
6. PRECAST PANEL
7. FAN COIL UNIT
8. GYPSUM WALL BOARD
9. ALUMINUM WINDOWS
10. GALVANIZED STEEL PRECAST CONNECTOR
11. SUSPENDED ACOUSTICAL CEILING

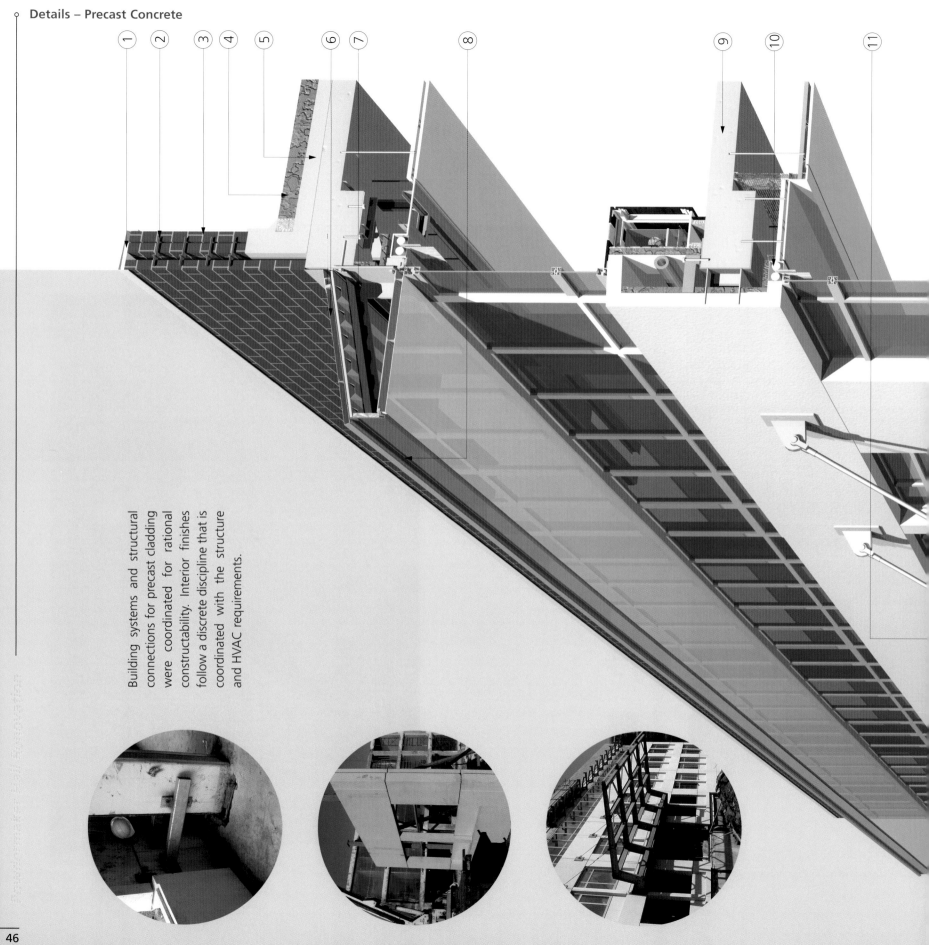

Building systems and structural connections for precast cladding were coordinated for rational constructability. Interior finishes follow a discrete discipline that is coordinated with the structure and HVAC requirements.

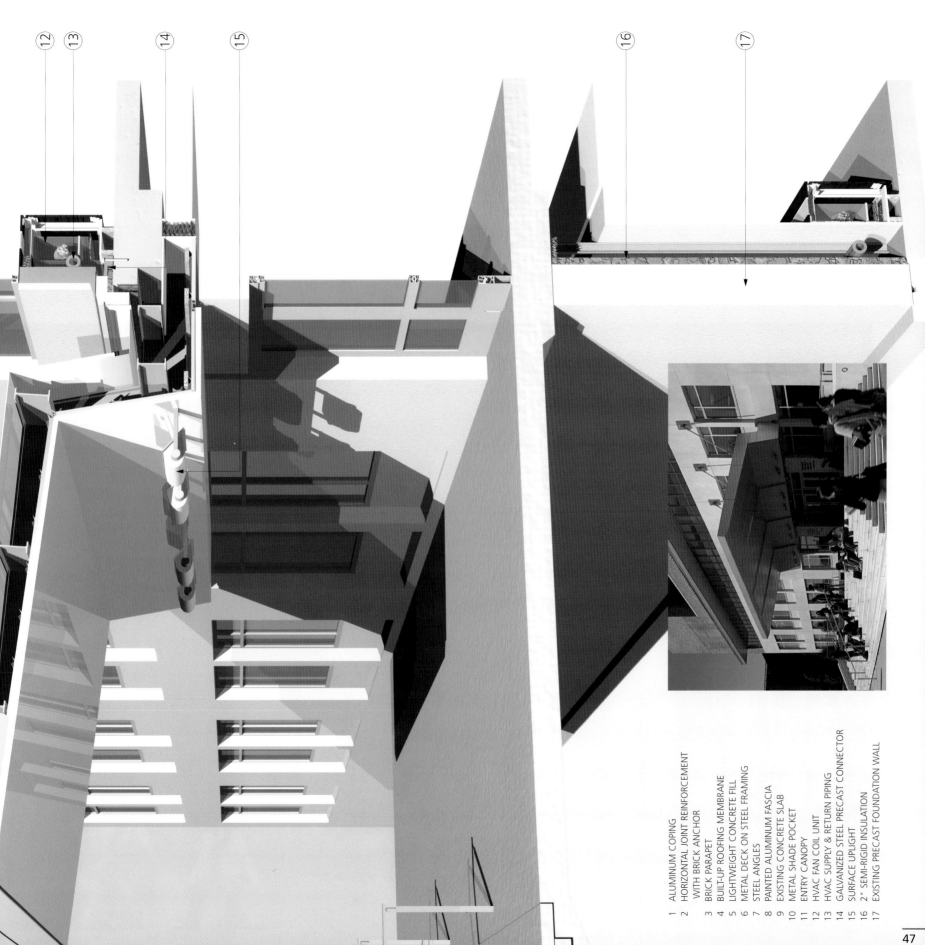

1 ALUMINUM COPING
2 HORIZONTAL JOINT REINFORCEMENT
  WITH BRICK ANCHOR
3 BRICK PARAPET
4 BUILT-UP ROOFING MEMBRANE
5 LIGHTWEIGHT CONCRETE FILL
6 METAL DECK ON STEEL FRAMING
7 STEEL ANGLES
8 PAINTED ALUMINUM FASCIA
9 EXISTING CONCRETE SLAB
10 METAL SHADE POCKET
11 ENTRY CANOPY
12 HVAC FAN COIL UNIT
13 HVAC SUPPLY & RETURN PIPING
14 GALVANIZED STEEL PRECAST CONNECTOR
15 SURFACE UPLIGHT
16 2" SEMI-RIGID INSULATION
17 EXISTING PRECAST FOUNDATION WALL

Before

Before

The views on these pages illustrate the use of precast cladding elements to mark special features, in this case, secondary building entrances.

A. Main lobby – looking in

B. Main lobby – looking out

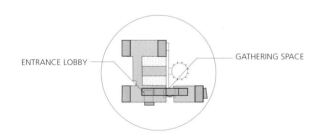

ENTRANCE LOBBY

GATHERING SPACE

C. Typical departmental suite

D. Plan – main lobby

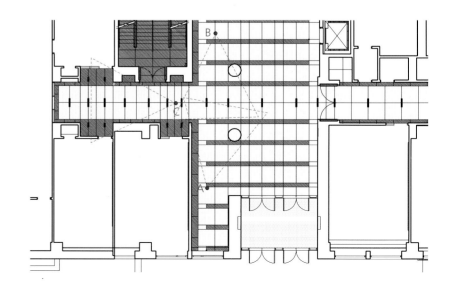

E. Student study lounge with commissioned artwork

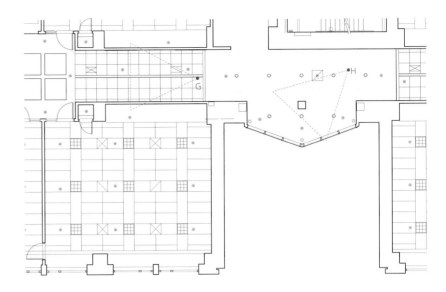

F. Plan – gathering space

Because of the corridors' extensive length (more than a quarter of a mile), they have been conceived of as village streets with a hierarchy of nodes and intersections. Nodes are at entries to classrooms, in clusters of three or four. Intersections are usually also resting/gathering places with seating and views to the outdoors.

Along the various itineraries is an extensive art installation of the works of two renowned photographers, commissioned for this project, Frank Gohlke and Joseph Sternfeld. They spent one year traveling through Queens together and independently to create a portfolio of 60 photographs, capturing the amazing cultural diversity, architecture and natural settings throughout the borough. Several quiet study rooms for commuter students include unique pieces created by artist Christian Philipp Müller.

Artist Julie Ault placed messages in the form of stainless steel letters at particular locations in the building, usually connected to points of entry. Her provocative statements are an apt transition from the outside world to the inside world of the intellect.

G. Classroom node along corridor

H. Gathering space near stair

Landscape

In contrast to the crisp coolness of the building interior, verdant landscaping is found in the two internal courtyards, providing sanctuary for building occupants. Designed by landscape artist Thomas Balsley and Associates, these spaces soften the view across from one wing to the other, creating a haven for wildlife and providing a veritable sacred space for quiet contemplation away from the sounds and crowds of the 12,000-student campus.

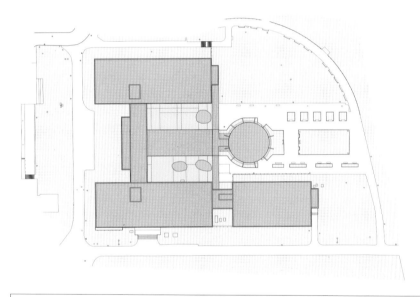

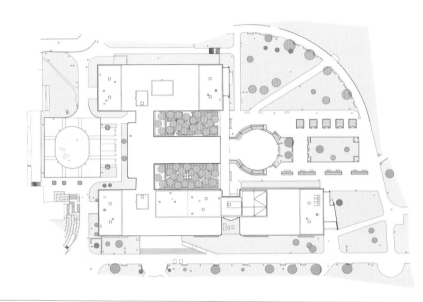

Landscape (Before)

Landscape (After)

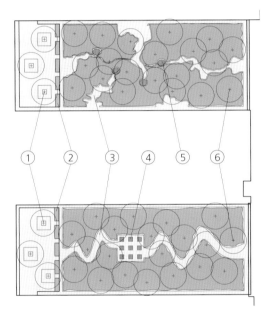

1   TREES PLANTED IN TREE PAVERS
2   WOODEN BENCH
3   WASHED RIVERSTONE
4   SPLIT-FACE UPRIGHT BOULDER
5   ROUNDED BOULDER
6   TREES IN PLANTING AREA

The demolition process removed hazardous materials, obsolete and deteriorated architectural, structural, and mechanical elements, preserving a rational structural grid, concrete floor and roof slabs, and internal stairs.

Attachments for a new prefabricated precast concrete wall system were adapted to the existing structure; panels were erected efficiently and windows easily snapped into place.

Mechanical penthouses and "background envelopes" are clad in hand-molded, hand-set brick in contrast to the precast concrete.

1991

1992

1993

1994

1995

1996

1997

1998

1999

2000

Concept Design
Schematic Design
Design Development

2001

Construction
Document

2002

Construction

2003

2004

2005

Completion

2006

NEW YORK COUNTY FAMILY COURT BUILDING RENOVATION
Dormitory Authority of the State of New York

New York, New York

New Program
Updated Program
Updated Circulation
New MEP Telecom System
Asbestos Removal
New Exterior Wall
Addition
Renovation

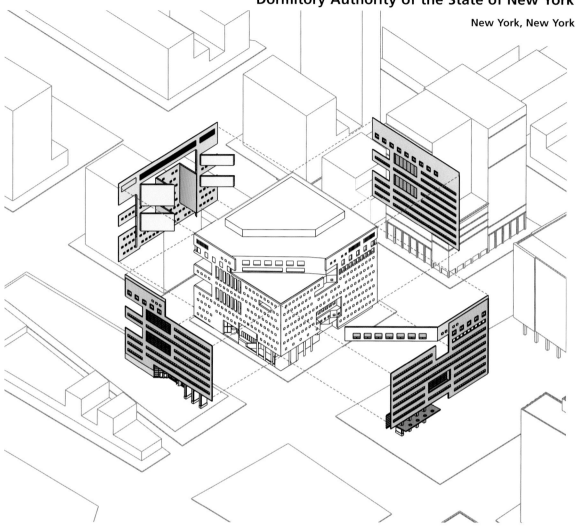

Designed in 1969, the New York County Family Court Building is a granite-clad civic structure in downtown Manhattan containing nearly 500,000 gross square feet of space. By the late 1990s, a number of serious deficiencies had arisen: a significant shortage of space within the building, the spaces provided were no longer adequate for their use, the mechanical systems were operating poorly, and the exterior cladding was coming loose from its anchorage.

Remedies completed since 1998 include an existing conditions survey, a space programming report, and mechanical upgrades and renovation. Underway is replacement of the building's envelope and a renovation of the entry and lobby spaces. Future work includes a renovation of the courtrooms on upper floors.

As a case study, the Courts renovation presents an intriguing example of how a Boomer Building is reborn through a series of iterative projects—all while the building has remained fully operational.

Building: 460,000 gross square feet
Cladding: 120,000 square feet
Lobby renovation: 15,000 gross square feet

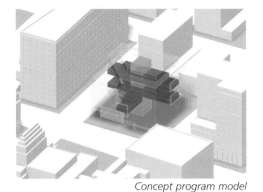

PRIMARY LOBBY

COURTROOM LOBBIES

PRIMARY CIRCULATION

Concept program model

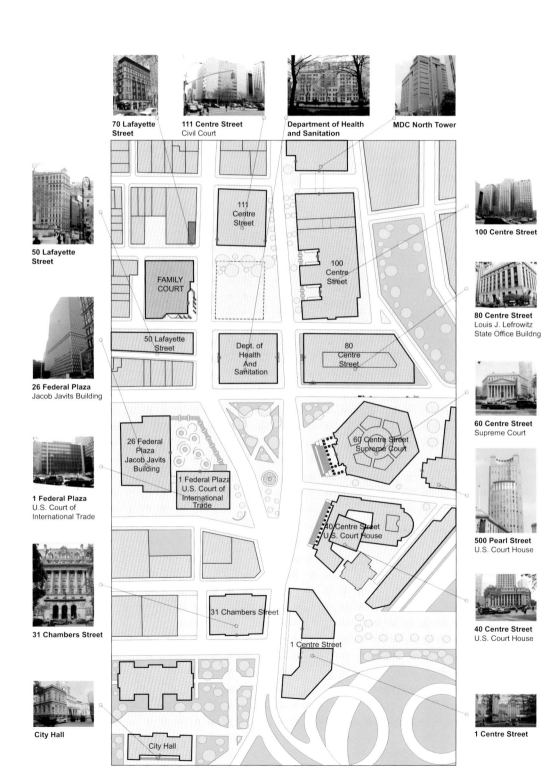

70 Lafayette Street

111 Centre Street
Civil Court

Department of Health and Sanitation

MDC North Tower

50 Lafayette Street

26 Federal Plaza
Jacob Javits Building

1 Federal Plaza
U.S. Court of International Trade

31 Chambers Street

City Hall

100 Centre Street

80 Centre Street
Louis J. Lefkowitz State Office Buildng

60 Centre Street
Supreme Court

500 Pearl Street
U.S. Court House

40 Centre Street
U.S. Court House

1 Centre Street

The Family Court Building is one of many structures that make up the Civic Court District in lower Manhattan. This district is an attractive blend of buildings, parks, and public plazas containing many distinguished structures housing city, state and federal agencies.

The buildings that make up this district vary in age and design, but many share certain qualities identified as unifying elements: use of light-colored stone, elements of architectural detail, and an architectural language that brings a certain dignity to the image of the buildings and the area. The Family Court Building, an unapologetic Brutalist structure, was largely lacking in these qualities.

Though the work undertaken focused on rectifying technical failures, the client also saw this as an opportunity to alter the image of the building, to make it more contextually sensitive.

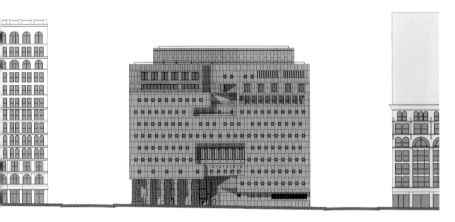

Lafayette Street facade (Before)

Lafayette Steet facade (After)

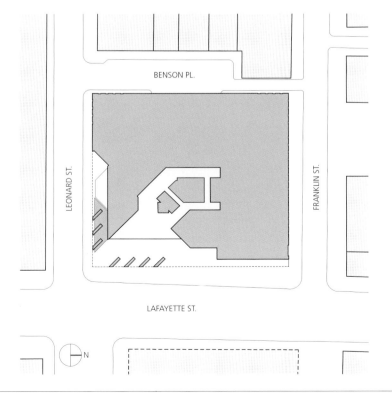

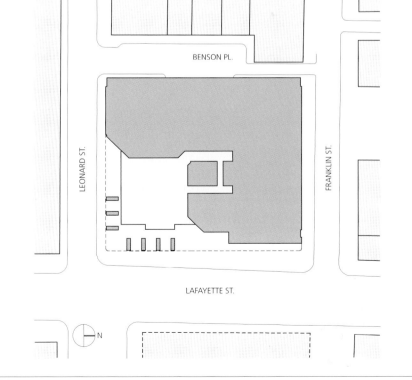

Lobby (Before)

Lobby (After)

Image

The Family Court Building had gained the reputation as a dark, foreboding structure. The architecture put an emphasis on formalism. Slices in the building created recessed areas in the mass, sometimes used for entrances and indications of significant program, other times purely for visual interest. The result was a building with many exterior areas in heavy shadow, with looming overhangs, often with columns that caused visual interference. Many inhabitants found the building menacing.

Stone cladding

The motivating factor in altering the exterior lay in the failure of the stone cladding. This failure was traced back to installation problems and the structural capability of the stone itself. One attempt had already been made at correcting the anchorage of the stone, so a redesign of the exterior cladding was seen as the best alternative.

.

Program

One particularly pressing programmatic need was the lobby. The Family Court system had changed markedly over the years and many more persons participate in proceedings than ever before. The lobby was half the size it needed to be. The renovation of the first floor focused on correcting this problem.

Thermal/Mechanical

This 1960s-vintage building was short on maintaining comfortable environmental conditions, particularly in the lobby, with its single-pane monolithic glass. The installation of one-inch-thick insulated glass would in itself significantly improve the thermal envelope.

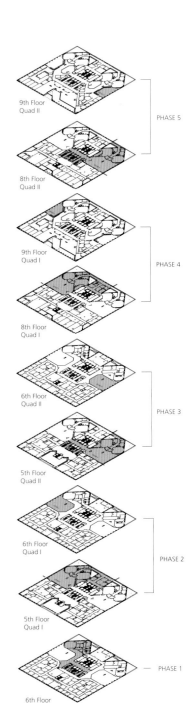

9th Floor
Quad II

8th Floor
Quad II

PHASE 5

9th Floor
Quad I

8th Floor
Quad I

PHASE 4

6th Floor
Quad II

5th Floor
Quad II

PHASE 3

6th Floor
Quad I

5th Floor
Quad I

PHASE 2

6th Floor

PHASE 1

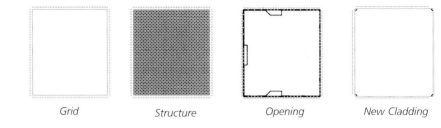

Grid   Structure   Opening   New Cladding

Structural model

The Family Court Building had existing conditions that the design team had little chance of altering. The structural system, like the Brutalist design, is inflexible and relentless. A cast-in-place concrete structure, the exterior wall is a 14-inch concrete shear wall. This condition highlighted the need to treat the facade as a thin veneer over an otherwise massive object.

The building design also relies heavily on a 3-foot 9-inch square grid that defines the size, proportion, and detailing of many of the spaces, window modules, and details. The design team found no economical alternative to depart from this grid.

Finally, the massing of the Family Court Building contains a variety of overpowering and capricious formal qualities. Mitchell | Giurgola focused on developing a hierarchy for these formal elements, with the intent of emphasizing some of the more rational aspects. One particularly troublesome design feature was the staggered pattern of punched windows on all facades.

Lafayette Street facade with cladding removed

Mitchell | Giurgola wanted to develop a light and tectonic facade. A detail at the corner of the building accentuates the granite face as a plane hovering in front of the mass of the building. At the corner, this granite mask rakes back from the edge to reveal the solid metal of the mass beneath.

A similar detail occurs at the top of the building, accentuating the granite outer plane and articulating the building as it meets the sky. The west facade required a different strategy entirely. This rear face has a plethora of cuts. Since there is little flat surface at the face of the building, the metal panels cover the entirety of this facade—a moment where the building is unmasked.

The large waiting areas on the upper floors provide natural light and views. Uninterrupted, double-height glass walls became the indicators of these spaces on the facade.

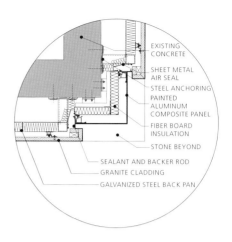

EXISTING CONCRETE

SHEET METAL AIR SEAL

STEEL ANCHORING

PAINTED ALUMINUM COMPOSITE PANEL

FIBER BOARD INSULATION

STONE BEYOND

SEALANT AND BACKER ROD

GRANITE CLADDING

GALVANIZED STEEL BACK PAN

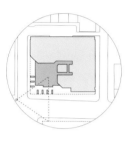

View from Lafayette Street

Unit mock-up

Embracing the notion of the cladding of the building as a skin, and recognizing the importance of delivering a technically sophisticated solution, the new cladding is a curtainwall.

A unitized curtainwall system is composed of repetitive, shop-manufactured units that can support stone, glass, and metal panels equally. The units are one floor high by one bay (3 feet, 9 inches) wide and are constructed of aluminum framing. Cladding materials hang on this rigid frame. The work in the field becomes a simple and repetitive connection between steel tabs on the curtainwall and steel clip angles on the concrete wall.

Granite is the preferred primary cladding material. The size of the stones is small and hung in a stacked joint pattern to accentuate a contemporary image. The window strip recessed from the plane of the wall establishes relief on the facade. Material choices within the window strip include metal sill panels, glass and metal spandrel panels, and vertical fins.

Scheme A1

Scheme A2

Scheme A3

Scheme B1

Scheme B2

Scheme B3

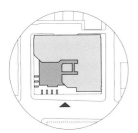

Design studies focused on moving away from a reading of the building as a solid cube and instead on a building with a light, thin, articulated skin.

Studies included an all-glass skin, while other options considered involved more contextual materials. These studies included two major investigations: a punched-window pattern and strips of recessed glazing. Spandrel glass, metal panel sills, and the depth of the window to add character and scale were studied. How the building meets the sky and the ground was important.

A number of changes modify the visual language of the structure. The heavy vertical columns that blocked major program spaces were removed. All but the largest setbacks were eliminated to regularize the facade. At the base of the building, columns set at a 45-degree angle to the facade were "turned" to open the entry and lobby to the street.

Stone panel with punched window

Glass panel

Stone panel with strip glazing

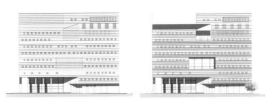

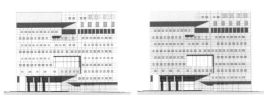
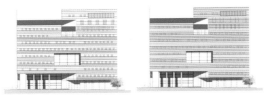

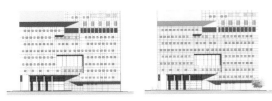
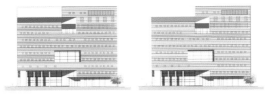

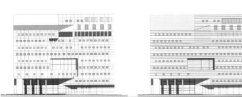
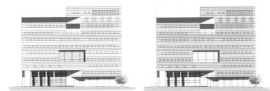

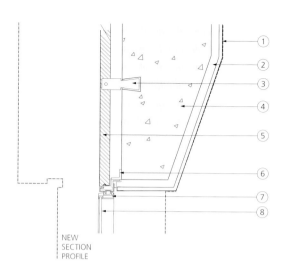

1. GYPSUM WALL BOARD
2. HAT CHANNEL FURRING
3. DOVETAIL STRAP IN CAST-IN-PLACE INSERT
4. CONCRETE BEAM
5. GRANITE FACE PANEL
6. SHELF ANGLE
7. EXTRUDED ALUMINUM OPERABLE WINDOW FRAME
8. GLAZING

East elevation (Before)

Wall section and head (Before)

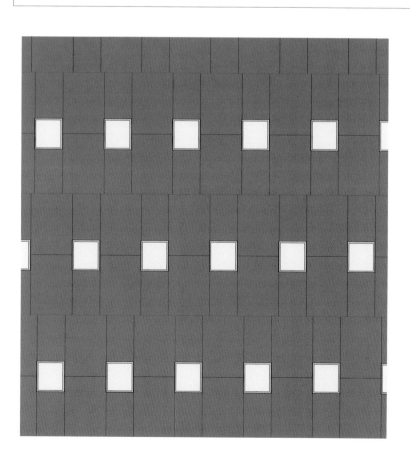

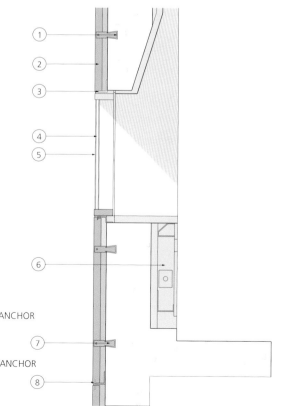

1. DOVETAIL SLOT
2. POLISHED GRANITE PANEL
3. CONTINUOUS GALVANIZED ANCHOR
4. POLISHED GLASS
5. PLATE TINTED GREY
6. FIN-TUBE RADIANT HEATER
7. STAINLESS DOVETAIL STRAP ANCHOR
8. STAINLESS STEEL DOWEL

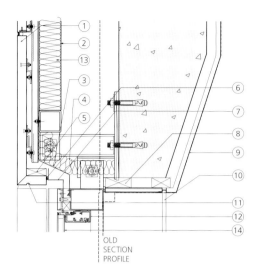

1. GRANITE CLADDING ON UNISTRUT STRUCTURAL SUPPORT
2. GALVANIZED STEEL BACK PAN
3. SHEET METAL AIR SEAL
4. MINERAL WOOL FIRESAFING
5. CONTINUOUS STONE BLOCKING
6. SEALANT AND BACKER ROD
7. PAINTED EXTRUDED ALUMINUM CLOSER
8. BLOCKING
9. PAINTED WALL BOARD
10. DOUBLE LEG REVEAL
11. PAINTED ALUMINUM OPERABLE WINDOW FRAME
12. CONTINUOUS DRIP EDGE
13. FOIL-FACED MINERAL WOOL INSULATION
14. STRUCTURALLY GLAZED INSULATED GLASS UNIT

OLD SECTION PROFILE

Wall section and head (New)

East elevation (New)

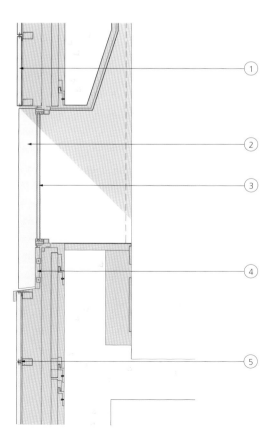

1. VENEER GRANITE PANELS ON UNITIZED ALUMINUM FRAME
2. VERTICAL GLASS FIN PRE-ATTACHED TO UNITIZED FRAME
3. OPERABLE ALUMINUM WINDOW PRE-ATTACHED TO UNTIZED FRAME
4. COMPOSITE ALUMINUM PANEL
5. 1/2" CAULK JOINT BETWEEN GRANITE PANELS

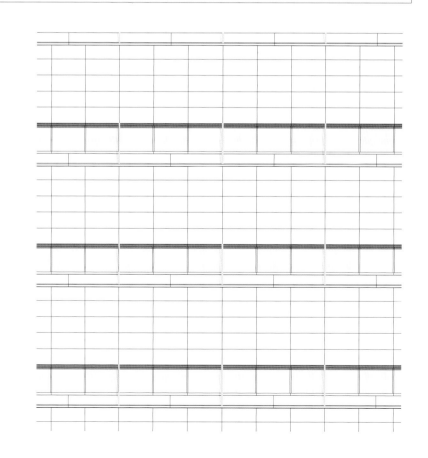

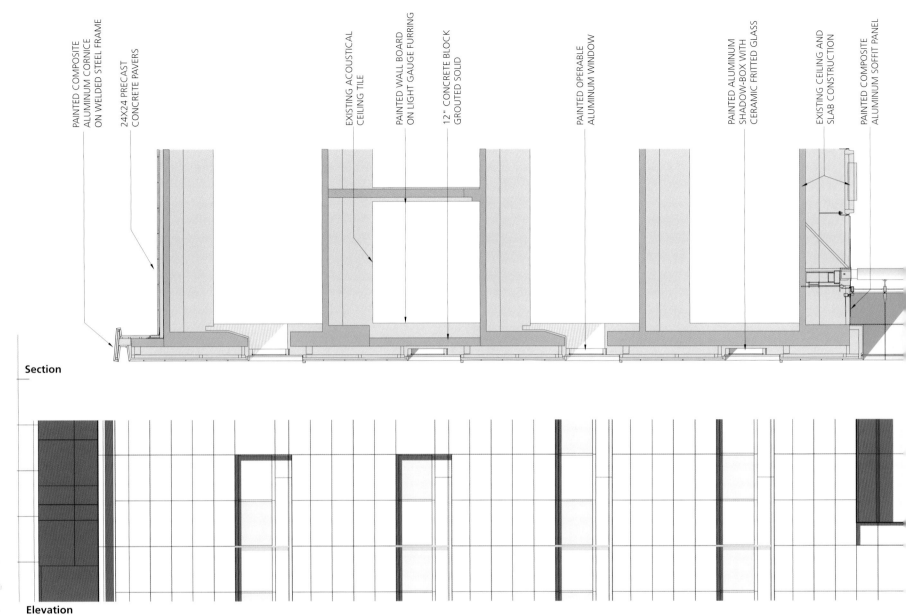

PAINTED COMPOSITE ALUMINUM CORNICE ON WELDED STEEL FRAME

24X24 PRECAST CONCRETE PAVERS

EXISTING ACOUSTICAL CEILING TILE

PAINTED WALL BOARD ON LIGHT GAUGE FURRING

12" CONCRETE BLOCK GROUTED SOLID

PAINTED OPERABLE ALUMINUM WINDOW

PAINTED ALUMINUM SHADOW-BOX WITH CERAMIC FRITTED GLASS

EXISTING CEILING AND SLAB CONSTRUCTION

PAINTED COMPOSITE ALUMINUM SOFFIT PANEL

Section

Elevation

Materials that introduce a more human scale to the building are given priority. Detailing these materials in a tectonic way brings scale and a second level of information to the building elements.

The granite (a gray-based stone from Georgia) makes a connection to the neighboring buildings. The textured stone achieves a richer degree of character when contrasted with the flat, clean look of the gray metal panels. Glass in various forms brings a soft translucent element to the palette. Vertical fins of low-iron glass with a translucent interlayer play rhythmically along the facade, while shadow-box spandrel panels lend depth to the areas of glazing.

Stainless steel accents the entrance canopy and main vestibule. The 25-foot-tall glass curtainwall is detailed with vertically butt-glazed joints, projected mullion caps, and cast stainless steel fittings and rods.

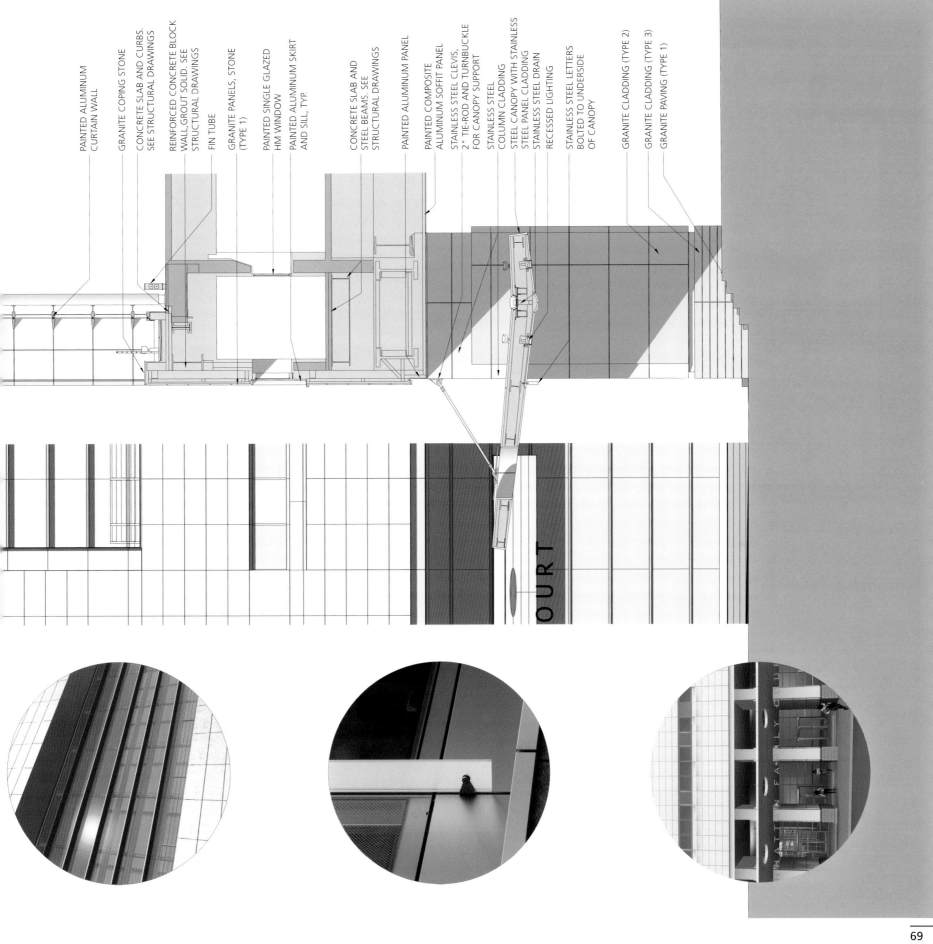

PAINTED ALUMINUM CURTAIN WALL

GRANITE COPING STONE

CONCRETE SLAB AND CURBS. SEE STRUCTURAL DRAWINGS

REINFORCED CONCRETE BLOCK WALL, GROUT SOLID. SEE STRUCTURAL DRAWINGS

FIN TUBE

GRANITE PANELS, STONE (TYPE 1)

PAINTED SINGLE GLAZED HM WINDOW

PAINTED ALUMINUM SKIRT AND SILL, TYP.

CONCRETE SLAB AND STEEL BEAMS. SEE STRUCTURAL DRAWINGS

PAINTED ALUMINUM PANEL

PAINTED COMPOSITE ALUMINUM SOFFIT PANEL

STAINLESS STEEL CLEVIS, 2" TIE-ROD AND TURNBUCKLE FOR CANOPY SUPPORT

STAINLESS STEEL COLUMN CLADDING

STEEL CANOPY WITH STAINLESS STEEL PANEL CLADDING

STAINLESS STEEL DRAIN

RECESSED LIGHTING

STAINLESS STEEL LETTERS BOLTED TO UNDERSIDE OF CANOPY

GRANITE CLADDING (TYPE 2)

GRANITE CLADDING (TYPE 3)

GRANITE PAVING (TYPE 1)

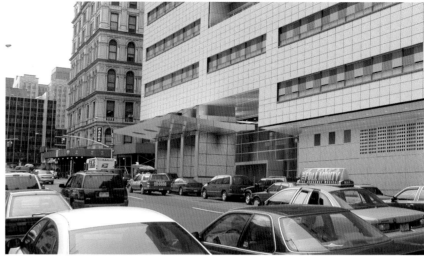

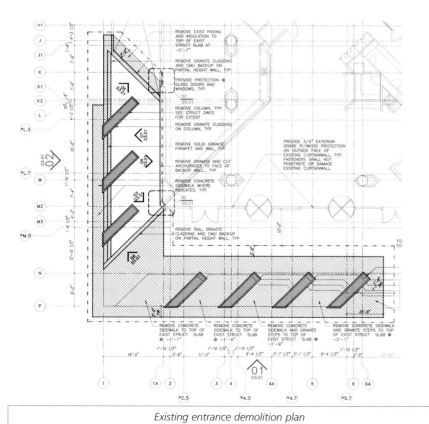

REMOVE EXIST PAVING AND INSULATION TO TOP OF EXIST STRUCT SLAB AT -0'-7"

REMOVE GRANITE CLADDING AND CMU BACKUP ON PARTIAL HEIGHT WALL, TYP

PROVIDE PROTECTION @ GLASS DOORS AND WINDOWS, TYP.

REMOVE COLUMN, TYP. SEE STRUCT DWGS FOR EXTENT

REMOVE GRANITE CLADDING ON COLUMN, TYP

REMOVE SOLID GRANITE PARAPET AND RAIL, TYP

REMOVE GRANITE AND CUT ANCHORAGES TO FACE OF BACKUP WALL, TYP

REMOVE CONCRETE SIDEWALK WHERE INDICATED, TYP.

PROVIDE 3/4" EXTERIOR GRADE PLYWOOD PROTECTION ON OUTSIDE FACE OF EXISTING CURTAINWALL, TYP. FASTENERS SHALL NOT PENETRATE OR DAMAGE EXISTING CURTAINWALL.

REMOVE RAIL, GRANITE CLADDING AND CMU BACKUP ON PARTIAL HEIGHT WALL, TYP

REMOVE CONCRETE SIDEWALK TO TOP OF EXIST STRUCT SLAB @ -1'-1"

REMOVE CONCRETE SIDEWALK TO TOP OF EXIST STRUCT SLAB @ -1'-4"

REMOVE CONCRETE SIDEWALK AND GRANITE STEPS TO TOP OF EXIST STRUCT SLAB @ -1'-9"

REMOVE CONCRETE SIDEWALK AND GRANITE STEPS TO TOP OF EXIST STRUCT SLAB @ -2'-1"

Existing entrance demolition plan

FOR AREA DRAIN PIPING AND SLEEVE DETAIL SEE PLUMBING DRAWINGS

PROVIDE SHEET MEMBRANE WATERPROOFING, PROTECTION BD, AND CRUSHED STONE OVER NEW AND EXISTING STRUCTURAL SLAB, TYP

TOP OF STRUCTURAL SLAB -0'-9"

PROVIDE CONTINUOUS 8'-0" HT. PTD PLYWOOD FENCE AT EXTENT OF PLAZA EXCAVATION

PROVIDE SHEET MEMBRANE WATERPROOFING, PROTECTION BD, AND CRUSHED STONE OVER NEW AND EXISTING STRUCTURAL SLAB, TYP

PIPE SLEEVE IMBEDDED IN COLUMN, TYP

TOP OF EXIST STRUCT SLAB -0'-9"

BACKFILL WITH COMPACTED SOIL. PROVIDE 5" CRUSHED STONE TOP SURFACE TO MATCH GRADE.

PROVIDE SHEET MEMBRANE WATERPROOFING, PROTECTION BD, CRUSHED STONE, BLOCKING, AND PRESSURE TREATED PLYWOOD TO MATCH GRADE OVER EXISTING AND NEW SLAB, TYP. SEE 10/A5.01 FOR DETAIL

TOP OF EXIST STRUCT SLAB -1'-1"

TOP OF EXIST STRUCT SLAB -1'-1"

TOP OF EXIST STRUCT SLAB -1'-9"

TOP OF EXIST STRUCT SLAB -2'-1"

New entrance plan

New York County Family Court Building Renovation

The original Court Building embraced the 45-degree angle at a profound level: the circulation pattern was based on it. The plan forced visitors into a canted direction that was disorienting and confused the clarity of passage though the structure.

Nowhere was this more evident than at the main entrance. Enormous, canted columns blocked, visually and physically, the main entry doors. Removing these major structural elements and inserting new columns perpendicular to the building exterior allowed for a more welcoming entry and ended the plague of the 45-degree angle at the front door. A significant new canopy brings a human, intimate, though still subtly monumental, scale to the entrance.

Lobby (Before)

Lobby (After)

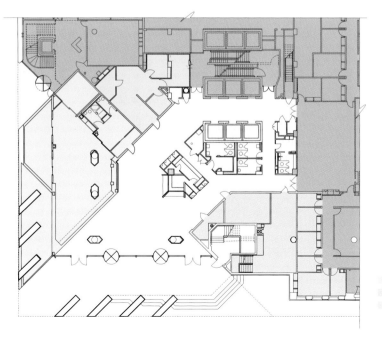

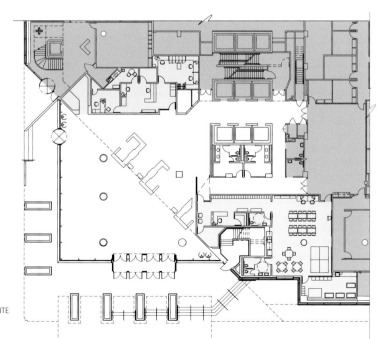

LOBBY
CHILDREN'S CENTER
OFFICE
COURT OFFICER'S SUITE

Augmenting these changes to the entrance sequence was the doubling of the lobby space. Aesthetically, the lobby is now a dynamic glass triangular volume that occupies the lower southeast corner of the building. With a clear view to the south and east, the lobby enjoys a visual connection with the surrounding buildings, as well as substantial amounts of natural light.

Programmatically, the enlarged lobby was made possible by the relocation of a city agency. This allowed a children's center and a security suite to remain directly adjacent to the primary lobby space. Bathrooms were redesigned to comply with ADA accessibility standards.

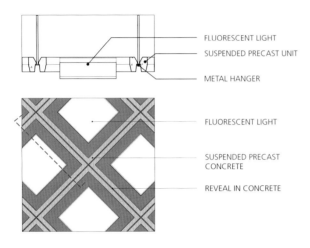

FLUORESCENT LIGHT

SUSPENDED PRECAST UNIT

METAL HANGER

FLUORESCENT LIGHT

SUSPENDED PRECAST CONCRETE

REVEAL IN CONCRETE

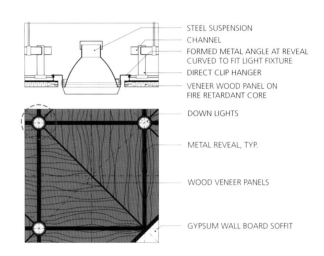

STEEL SUSPENSION CHANNEL

FORMED METAL ANGLE AT REVEAL CURVED TO FIT LIGHT FIXTURE

DIRECT CLIP HANGER

VENEER WOOD PANEL ON FIRE RETARDANT CORE

DOWN LIGHTS

METAL REVEAL, TYP.

WOOD VENEER PANELS

GYPSUM WALL BOARD SOFFIT

| *Reflected ceiling plan (Before)* | *Reflected ceiling plan (After)* |

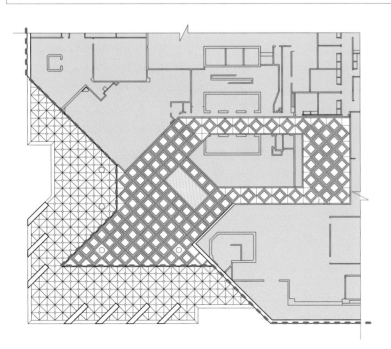

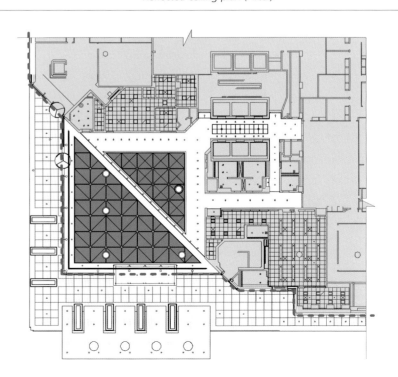

New York County Family Court Building Renovation

The design work on the interior focused on creating a more humane, logical and dignified environment. Materials include buff-colored limestone walls, Makore wood ceilings, terrazzo floors with gray, buff, and blue tones, and bead-blasted stainless steel trim.

As an example, the original ceiling and lighting detail included a plodding grid of heavy, square, precast concrete rings that loomed overhead. These rings surrounded a two-foot-square lay-in light fixture that floated in dark, open space.

The new ceiling design uses large panels of quarter-sawn Makore, a reddish-brown wood, as the primary ceiling material. The panels are designed as triangular units that both embrace and play with the grid pattern. Lighting is incorporated into this pattern at the intersections and uses translucent baffles to reflect light back onto the wood surface.

 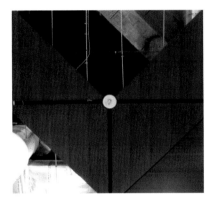 

The unitized curtainwall is a rigid frame of 6-inch-deep extruded aluminum mullions that support individual pieces of stone, metal and glass. The stone, Oconee granite, was removed in blocks from a central Georgia quarry and shipped to a stone fabricator for slabbing, cutting and finishing. The individual stone units, at one and a half inches thick, were sent to the curtainwall fabricator for assembly onto rigid frames. Metal panels, vision and spandrel insulated glass units, and glass fins were also installed onto these 13-foot-high x 3-foot, 9-inch units in a controlled shop environment. The units were then individually crated and shipped to the project site. Final installation proceeded on a unit-by-unit basis, off a swing-scaffold, in a top-to-bottom, left-to-right sequence.

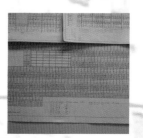

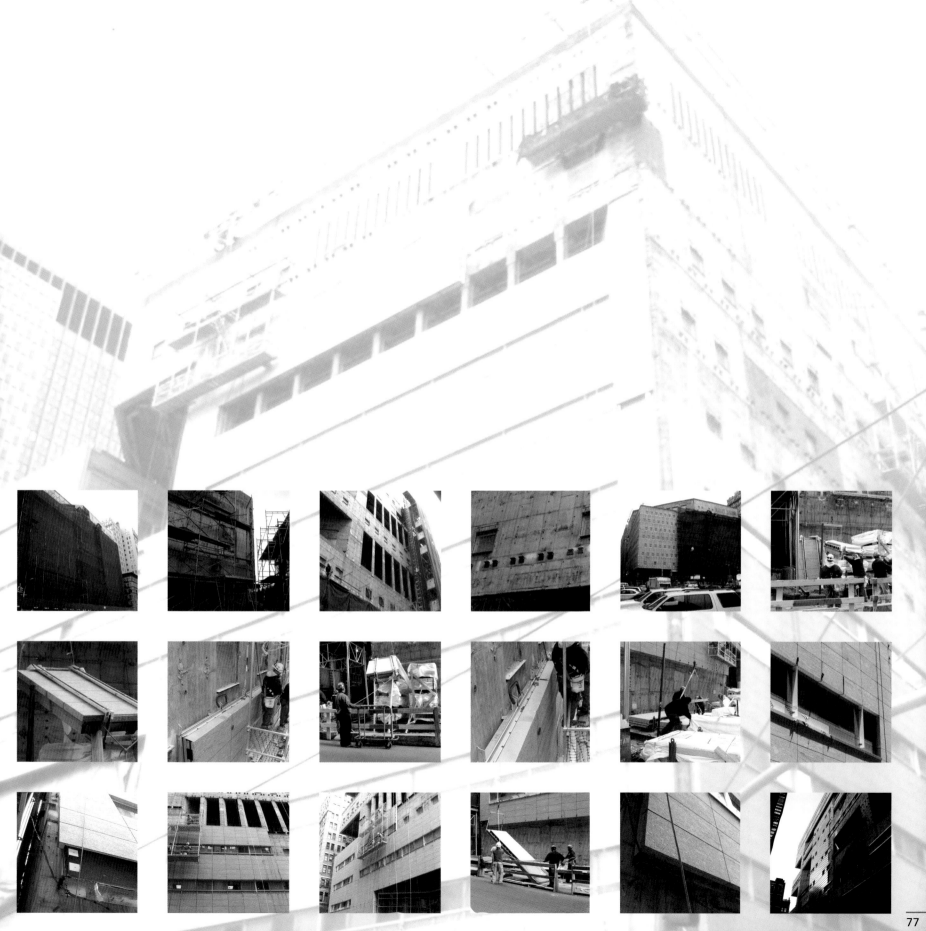

Interior Renovation/New Addition

- Boyd Hall Addition and Renovation

- New Science Building Renovation and Addition

1991

1992

1993

1994

1995

1996

1997

1998

1999

Concept Design

2000

Schematic Design

Design Development

2001

Construction
Document

2002

Construction

2003

Completion

2004

2005

2006

BOYD HALL ADDITION AND RENOVATION
Plymouth State University Department of Natural Science

Plymouth, New Hampshire

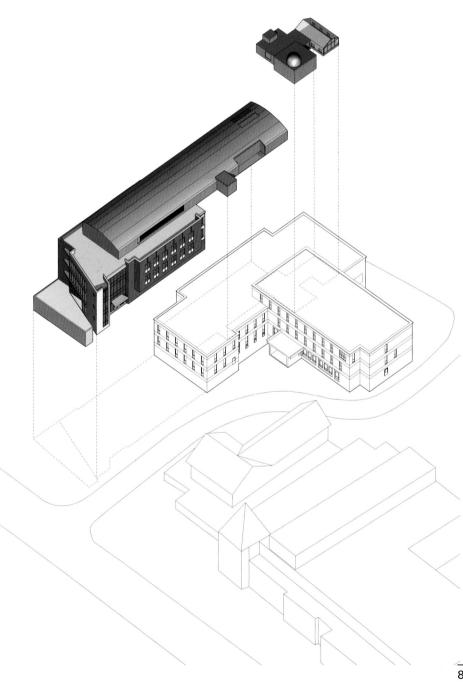

Boyd Hall was constructed in 1969 as a multipurpose classroom building for the sciences. Thirty years later, it no longer met the educational needs of the college. The building illustrates the shortcomings of that vintage of science building. It had inadequate ventilation, no air conditioning, and low floor-to-floor height that would complicate the installation of new ductwork. The building's mechanical and electrical systems and equipment were outdated, energy inefficient, and in need of complete replacement. The lighting was poor, and the building lacked such basic research needs as a centralized pure water system, glass-washing facilities, and adequate fume hoods. The casework and finishes were worn out and in need of replacement. One's overall impression when entering the building was that science was a grim pursuit, and not much changed in 30 years.

Boyd Hall's deficiencies, coupled with the increasing importance of science programs at Plymouth State, led to the programming and design of the renovation of the existing facility and the design of a new addition. The combined facility houses the Natural Science Department, which includes the following disciplines: Biology, Chemistry, Meteorology, Physical Science, and Science Education. The program also includes the Mark E. Sylvestre Planetarium, the New England Weather Technology Evaluation Center, department offices, and the 220-seat Boyd Auditorium. In addition to the wide range of laboratories the building also contains equipment and facilities unusual for an undergraduate laboratory such as an electron microscope, nuclear magnetic resonance spectrometer, animal facilities for rodents and lobsters, a TV studio for weather reporting, and a rooftop greenhouse and observatory.

Area: 90,000 total gross square feet
35,600 square feet addition
54,400 square feet renovation

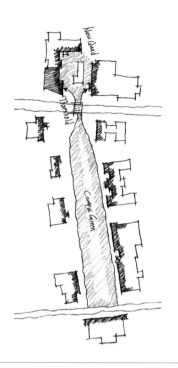

The site of Boyd Hall was set back from the main road behind a parking lot and was difficult to access, creating a physical disconnection from the main campus. The placement of the addition over the surface parking lot presented the opportunity to create a new quad and to establish a prominent place for the sciences on the campus. An adjacent new library, recently completed, successfully defines one edge of the quad. But Boyd Hall lacked presence and failed to adequately define the other edge. The addition is north of the existing Boyd Hall, reinforcing this edge and completing the new quad with a strong entrance and dynamic gathering space at the arrival point. The addition connects the science building to the campus, heralding the importance of science to the academic and local community.

The front face of the building slightly angles to the east as a gesture to the town of Plymouth and to take advantage of the spectacular views of the White Mountains.

Campus plan

Existing site plan

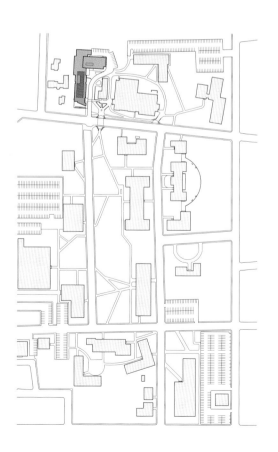

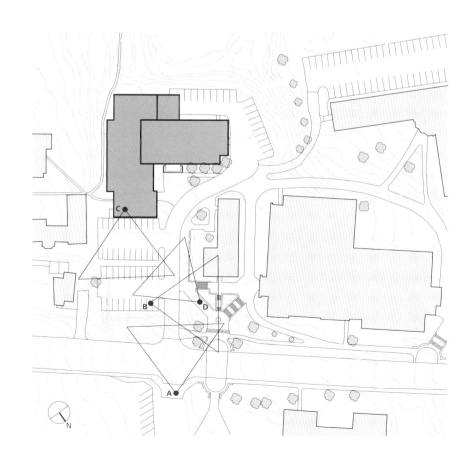

View A

View B

View C

View D

New site plan

Site intervention diagram

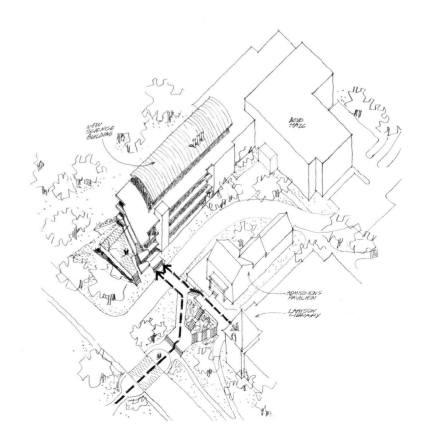

The treatment of the face of the building on the north addition is crucial because it represents the science facility to both the campus and the town.

The decision was made to put the public elements of the program in the front of the addition. The campus-wide lecture room and adjoining lobby and outdoor courtyard, the seminar rooms, and the staircase all face the campus, mountain views, and the town. The lounge and staircase windows face the library and entrance, creating a dialogue with the new quad.

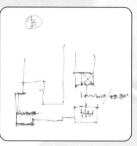

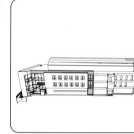

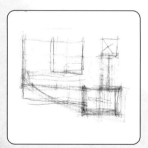

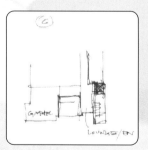

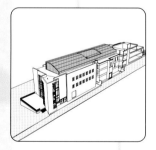

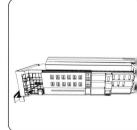

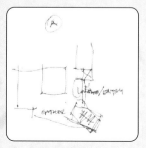

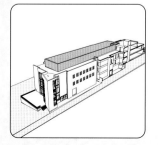

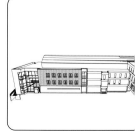

Site alternatives	*Concept sketch*	*Front corner*	*Penthouse*	*Parapet*

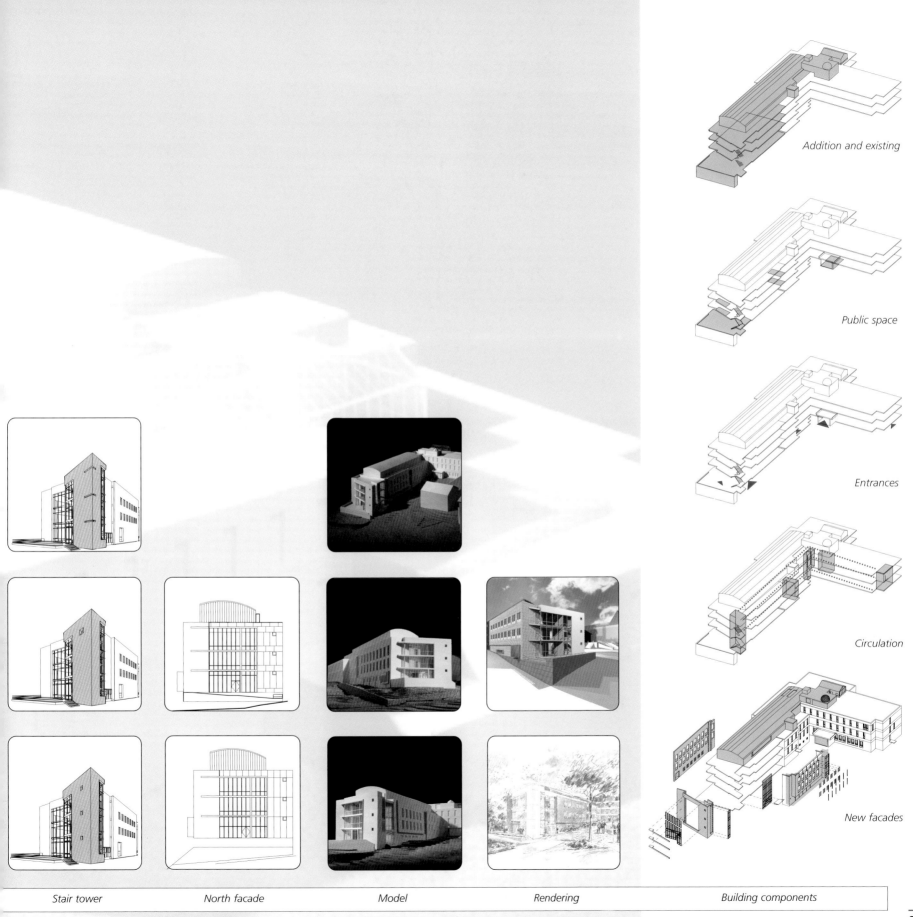

Stair tower

North facade

Model

Rendering

Building components

Addition and existing

Public space

Entrances

Circulation

New facades

| Existing plan | New plan | *PROGRAM* |

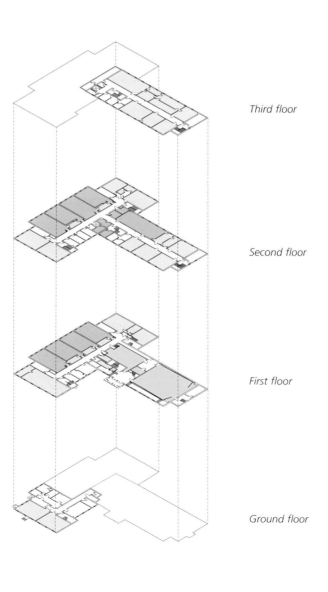

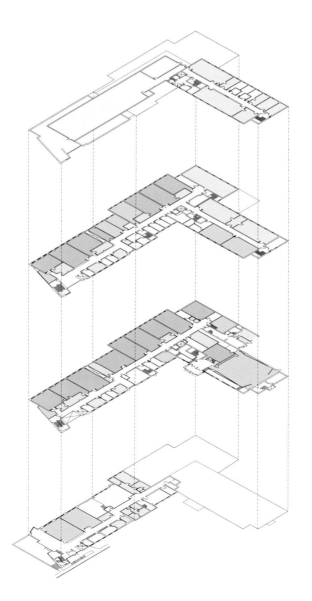

Third floor

Second floor

First floor

Ground floor

CLASSROOM
LABS
CIRCULATION
OFFICE
SHARED
SUPPORT

The addition to the north of the existing building allows for consistent programming within the two wings. The lab facilities continue in the north wing through the addition, and the classrooms remain in the west wing. The new mechanical penthouse sits atop both elements of the north wing. The continuous lab space in the old and new portions of the north wing allows the mechanical penthouse to serve the areas where supply and exhaust requirements are the heaviest.

Boyd Hall is typical of academic buildings constructed in the 1960s and early 1970s and shares many of the same problems as buildings of its era. The 30-plus-year-old building systems have exceeded their anticipated service lives and no longer conform to contemporary energy and air quality standards. Boyd Hall had a tight floor-to-distribution system. The low floor-to-floor height

created the need to minimize ductwork crossovers. For the renovation, the air supply and return systems for the labs remain independent from those for the classrooms and offices to minimize crossover of the ducts. The red ducts shown in the diagram represent the primary supplier to the labs, which run through the center of the ceiling. Additional air handlers, supplying the blue and green ducts in the diagram, service the classrooms, offices, the main lecture room, and corridors from a separate shaft.

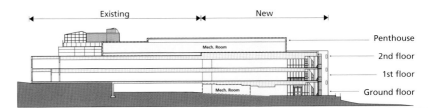

| MEP | Existing MEP | New MEP system |

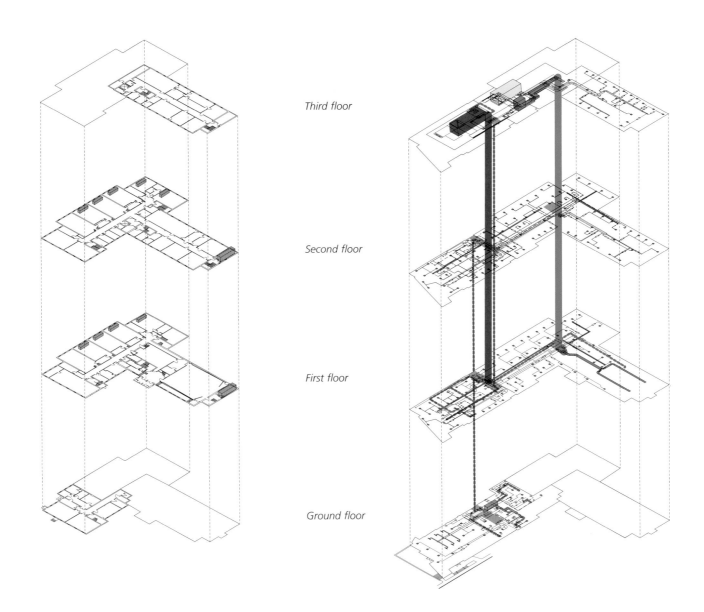

Third floor

Second floor

First floor

Ground floor

■ AHU 1
▨ AHU 2
■ AHU 3
■ AHU 4
  AHU 5
--- AIR RETURN

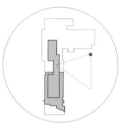

The new double-height glass entry of the addition enhances the sense of arrival and creates a dialogue with the library entry. Its masonry facade, with vertically accented punched windows, establishes continuity with Boyd Hall, while the white spandrel panels echo the horizontality of Boyd's concrete banding.

New | Existing

West elevation

One of the overarching goals of the project was to create a dynamic new image for the sciences. The new addition provided this opportunity. The lab/office element is enclosed in brick to complement the brick of the original building and neighboring admissions building and new library project, achieving a balanced integration of old and new. The public face on the north wing that houses the common areas (lecture room lobby, stairwell, seminar rooms) is clad in precast concrete and glass to differentiate itself from the program of the lab/classroom wings. The vertical emphasis on the window treatment of the addition complements the vertical fenestration of the existing building. Both the large glazed glass curtainwall on the public face and the cutout windows facing the quad echo this verticality.

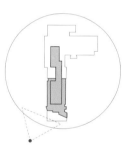

Recessive entries were a hallmark of many Boomer Buildings, and Boyd Hall is no exception. The new addition not only provided the opportunity to place the entrance to the new facility in a more prominent and convenient location, but also to enhance its scale and presence. The new entry is entirely glazed and open to the upper level, creating a welcoming and inviting feel to its occupants.

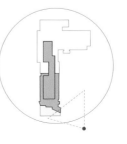

The enclosure of the addition is made energy efficient through the use of high-performance spray-applied polyurethane foam insulation and insulated glazing with warm edge spacers. Vertical fins on the east and west windows provide solar shading. New insulated glass windows are provided in Boyd Hall, as well.

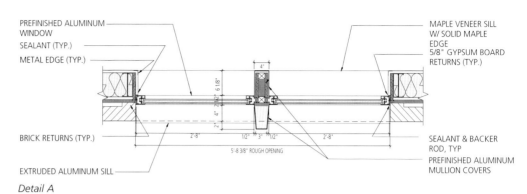

PREFINISHED ALUMINUM WINDOW
SEALANT (TYP.)
METAL EDGE (TYP.)
MAPLE VENEER SILL W/ SOLID MAPLE EDGE
5/8" GYPSUM BOARD RETURNS (TYP.)
BRICK RETURNS (TYP.)
EXTRUDED ALUMINUM SILL
SEALANT & BACKER ROD, TYP
PREFINISHED ALUMINUM MULLION COVERS

5'-8 3/8" ROUGH OPENING
2'-8"   1/2"   3"   1/2"   2'-8"
4"
2 1/2" 2 1/2" 4" 6 1/8"

Detail A

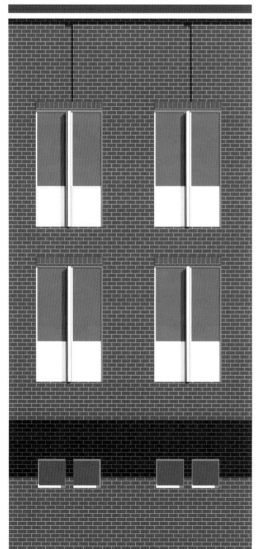

West elevation (New)

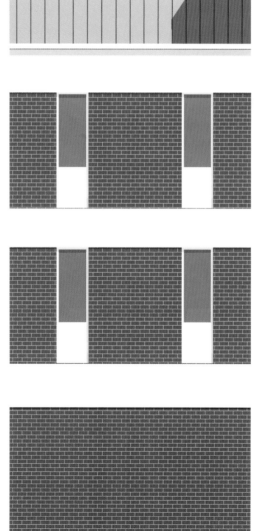

West elevation (Existing)

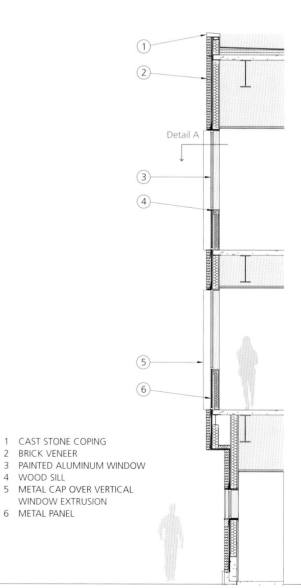

1 CAST STONE COPING
2 BRICK VENEER
3 PAINTED ALUMINUM WINDOW
4 WOOD SILL
5 METAL CAP OVER VERTICAL WINDOW EXTRUSION
6 METAL PANEL

Detail A

Wall section

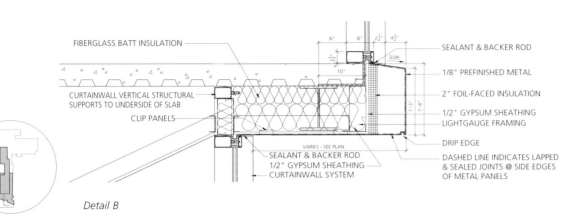

FIBERGLASS BATT INSULATION

CURTAINWALL VERTICAL STRUCTURAL
SUPPORTS TO UNDERSIDE OF SLAB

CLIP PANELS

SEALANT & BACKER ROD
1/2" GYPSUM SHEATHING
CURTAINWALL SYSTEM

SEALANT & BACKER ROD

1/8" PREFINISHED METAL

2" FOIL-FACED INSULATION

1/2" GYPSUM SHEATHING
LIGHTGAUGE FRAMING

DRIP EDGE

DASHED LINE INDICATES LAPPED
& SEALED JOINTS @ SIDE EDGES
OF METAL PANELS

SLOPE

VARIES - SEE PLAN

Detail B

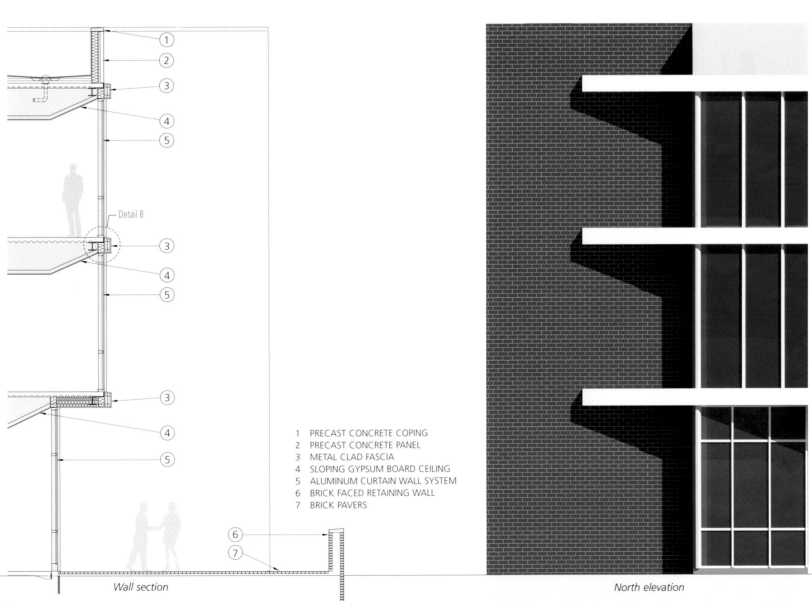

Detail B

1   PRECAST CONCRETE COPING
2   PRECAST CONCRETE PANEL
3   METAL CLAD FASCIA
4   SLOPING GYPSUM BOARD CEILING
5   ALUMINUM CURTAIN WALL SYSTEM
6   BRICK FACED RETAINING WALL
7   BRICK PAVERS

Wall section

North elevation

The original Boyd Hall, like many Boomer Buildings, lacked public amenity spaces. The new addition rectifies this situation by providing a generous lobby and outdoor terrace off the campus-wide lecture room, a lounge area overlooking student activity in the newly created quad entrance, and study "nooks" at the junction between the new and existing building.

A. Public lobby off lecture room located in north addition, with entrance to outdoor terrace

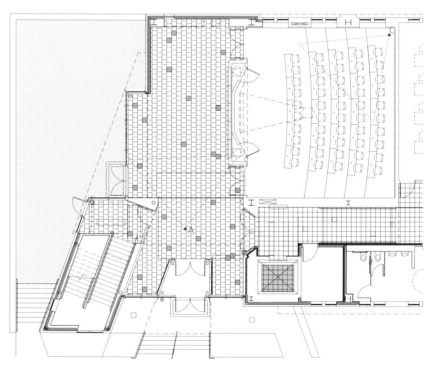

Floor plan of entry lobby and lecture room

B. View of Quad through large curtainwall glass from top floor of two-story lobby

C. Campus wide multimedia lecture room

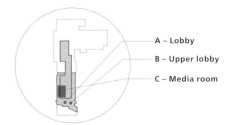

A – Lobby

B – Upper lobby

C – Media room

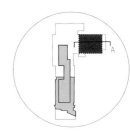

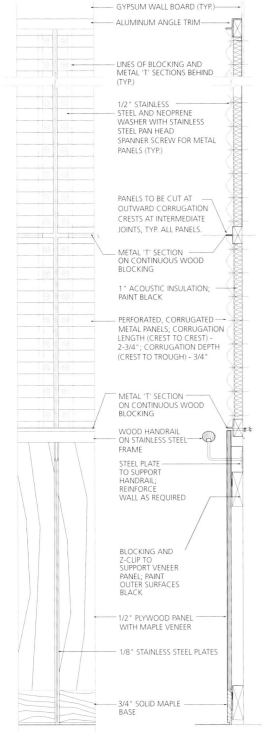

GYPSUM WALL BOARD (TYP.)

ALUMINUM ANGLE TRIM

LINES OF BLOCKING AND
METAL 'T' SECTIONS BEHIND
(TYP.)

1/2" STAINLESS
STEEL AND NEOPRENE
WASHER WITH STAINLESS
STEEL PAN HEAD
SPANNER SCREW FOR METAL
PANELS (TYP.)

PANELS TO BE CUT AT
OUTWARD CORRUGATION
CRESTS AT INTERMEDIATE
JOINTS, TYP. ALL PANELS.

METAL 'T' SECTION
ON CONTINUOUS WOOD
BLOCKING

1" ACOUSTIC INSULATION;
PAINT BLACK

PERFORATED, CORRUGATED
METAL PANELS; CORRUGATION
LENGTH (CREST TO CREST) -
2-3/4"; CORRUGATION DEPTH
(CREST TO TROUGH) - 3/4"

METAL 'T' SECTION
ON CONTINUOUS WOOD
BLOCKING

WOOD HANDRAIL
ON STAINLESS STEEL
FRAME

STEEL PLATE
TO SUPPORT
HANDRAIL;
REINFORCE
WALL AS REQUIRED

BLOCKING AND
Z-CLIP TO
SUPPORT VENEER
PANEL; PAINT
OUTER SURFACES
BLACK

1/2" PLYWOOD PANEL
WITH MAPLE VENEER

1/8" STAINLESS STEEL PLATES

3/4" SOLID MAPLE
BASE

B. Interior wall section

Auditorium (Before)

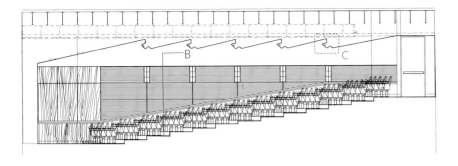

A. Auditorium – sectional elevation

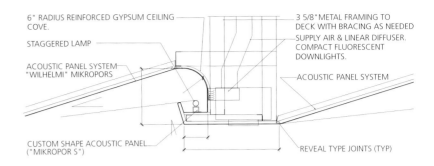

6" RADIUS REINFORCED GYPSUM CEILING COVE.

STAGGERED LAMP

ACOUSTIC PANEL SYSTEM "WILHELMI" MIKROPORS

CUSTOM SHAPE ACOUSTIC PANEL ("MIKROPOR S")

3 5/8" METAL FRAMING TO DECK WITH BRACING AS NEEDED

SUPPLY AIR & LINEAR DIFFUSER. COMPACT FLUORESCENT DOWNLIGHTS.

ACOUSTIC PANEL SYSTEM

REVEAL TYPE JOINTS (TYP)

C. Auditorium – ceiling detail

Auditorium (After)

The interior renovation of Boyd Hall faced the same challenges of creating a seamless integration between the old and the new building. The goal of the design team was to upgrade the existing facilities to match the finishes, the systems, and the technology of the new facilities. The renovated 220-seat auditorium, located on the ground floor of the west wing, was enhanced by a perforated brushed aluminum panel (see wall section detail) and acoustical treatment with a state-of-the-art audiovisual system. An indirect cove lighting system with recessed fluorescents and continuous slot diffusers (refer to sectional elevation and ceiling detail) replaces the suspended fluorescent fixtures. Similar materials and details are used in the new lecture hall to create a unity between the old and new.

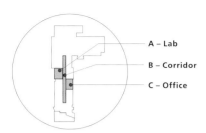

A – Lab
B – Corridor
C – Office

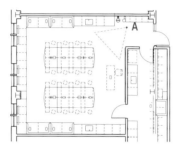

A

The new facility includes labs, classrooms, offices, and support rooms that provide functional, technically advanced spaces to attract faculty and students to the programs housed in Boyd Hall. The teaching and research labs accommodate current and changing technology. Lab benches and storage cabinets consist of maple veneer and epoxy resin countertops. Non-lab areas use plastic laminate. The lecture room has a computer work area behind the lecture rows allowing for flexibility in teaching. Niches created within the corridors near the labs provide gathering spaces to the entrance. The pinup space and accent colors in the corridor have an inviting feel. Labs and classrooms feature pendant light fixtures and blackout shades for full audio-visual light control; offices have recessed light fixtures.

Boyd Hall Addition and Renovation

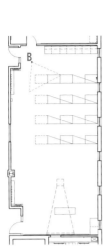

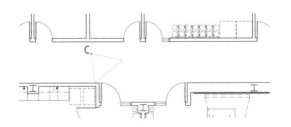

Construction

The choice to completely renovate and add on to Boyd Hall rather than demolishing it and building anew resulted in a 90,000-square-foot advanced facility constructed at a cost of $153 per square foot, compared to $213 per square foot for a new building. It also accommodated an accelerated construction schedule, allowing the science department to reoccupy the building within a one-year academic time frame.

Construction completion July 2003
Occupant move in July 2003
Class start August 2003

May 2002   Occupant move out
Construction Start Renovation
Construction Start Addition

08/24/2002

09/12/2002

10/09/2002

11/25/2002

12/04/2002

08/03/2003

06/02/2003

04/27/2003

04/07/2003

03/04/2003

12/19/2002

12/28/2002

01/05/2003

02/12/2003

02/23/2003

1991

1992

1993

1994

1995

1996

1997

1998

1999

2000

2001

2002
Concept Design

Schematic Design

Design Development

2003
Construction
Document
Construction

2004

Completion

2005

2006

NEW SCIENCE BUILDING RENOVATION AND ADDITION
Keene State College Department of Natural Science

Keene, New Hampshire

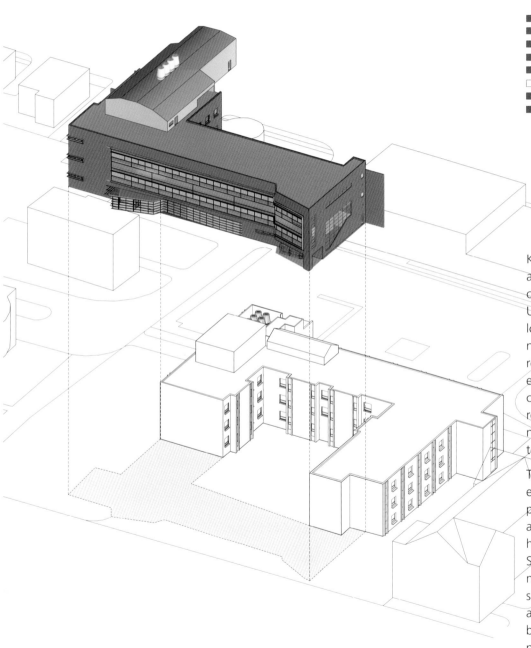

- ■ New Program
- ■ Updated Program
- ■ Updated Circulation
- ■ New MEP Telecom System
- ■ Asbestos Removal
- □ New Exterior Wall
- ■ Addition
- ■ Renovation

Keene State College constructed the Science Building in 1967, and 33 years later it no longer met the educational needs of the college. Like its counterpart, Boyd Hall at Plymouth State University, it had inadequate ventilation, no air conditioning, and low floor-to-floor height that would complicate the installation of new ductwork. The building lacked such basic research requirements as a centralized pure water system, a centralized lab exhaust system, and an adequate number of fume hoods. The lab casework and finishes were worn out and in need of replacement. The building simply did not meet the standards necessary to attract students to the sciences, which were moving to the forefront of the College's academic agenda.

The Sciences Building's deficiencies, coupled with the need for expanded state-of-the-art teaching laboratory space, led to the programming and design of the renovation of the existing facility and the design of the new addition. The combined facility now houses Biology, Chemistry, Physics, Geology, Environmental Science, Geography, Mathematics, and Computer Science. The new addition accommodates large 40-seat classrooms and a 110-seat, sloped floor multimedia lecture room, which are shared by all disciplines. In addition to the wide range of laboratories, the building also contains equipment and facilities growing in popularity for undergraduate study, such as an NMR facility as well as laser and optics labs.

Area: 93,640 gross square feet
         38,527 square feet addition
         55,113 square feet renovation

Context and Site

The existing Science Building was located in the heart of the academic campus on its central circulation spine, known locally as the "Appian Way" after the Ancient Roman road. Its U-shaped configuration provided minimal contact with pedestrian circulation while allowing the walkway to "leak" into an ill-defined courtyard. The main entry was sandwiched between two bulbous, masonry-clad lecture halls.

The new addition was an opportunity to create a strong presence for the Science Department on the Appian Way and integrate the building into the campus fabric. The functionally obsolete tiered lecture halls were demolished and replaced with a three-story, L-shaped addition that connects the legs of the existing building, creates a new enclosed courtyard, and provides a continuous face with two strong entry points along the Appian Way. A glazed circulation gallery for accessing the lecture room faces the Appian Way, while on the second and third floors, the galleries to the labs face the courtyard.

The vocabulary of red brick and white-metal-framed glazing found in the adjacent student center and library across the way is used for the new addition.

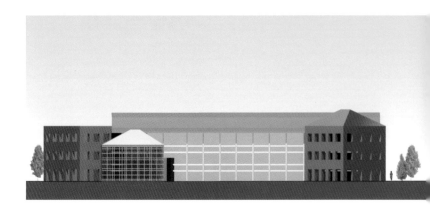

Campus plan	Context elevation

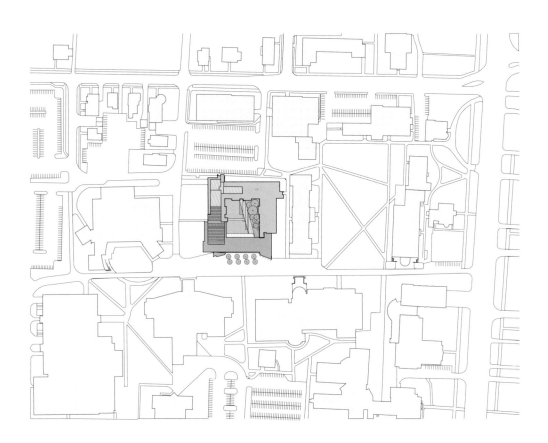

View A

View B

View C

View D

Existing site plan

New site plan

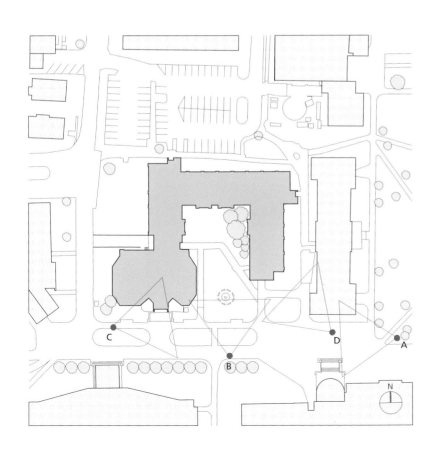

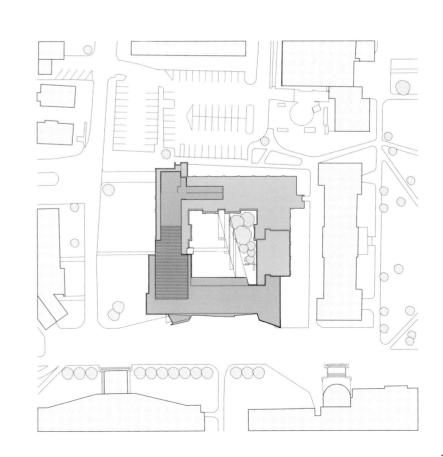

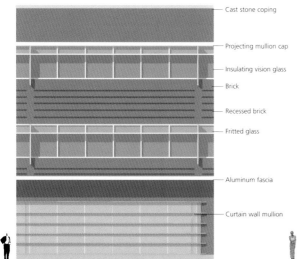

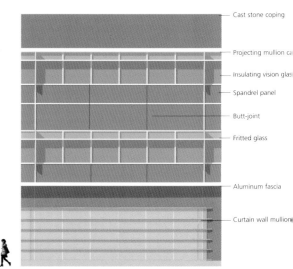

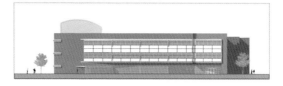

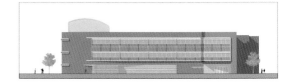

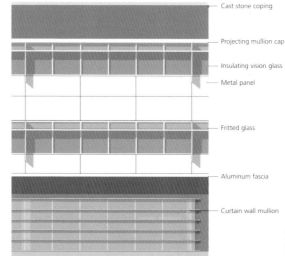

Cast stone coping

Projecting mullion cap

Insulating vision glass

Brick

Recessed brick

Fritted glass

Aluminum fascia

Curtain wall mullion

Cast stone coping

Projecting mullion cap

Insulating vision glass

Metal panel

Fritted glass

Aluminum fascia

Curtain wall mullion

Cast stone coping

Projecting mullion cap

Insulating vision glass

Spandrel panel

Butt-joint

Fritted glass

Aluminum fascia

Curtain wall mullion

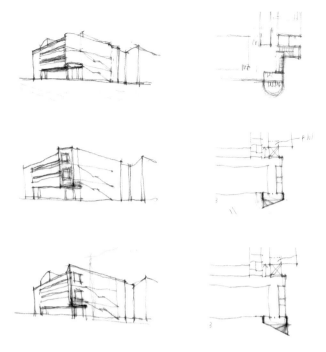

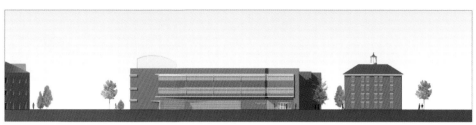

A1 Glass window with brick spandrel

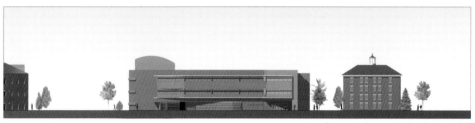

A2 Glass window with brick spandrel

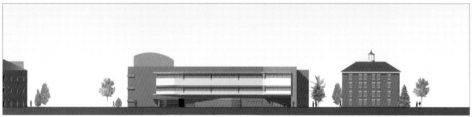

B1 Glass window with metal spandrel

The south-facing addition presented an opportunity to maximize daylighting in the labs while controlling solar heat gain through the use of passive solar-shading devices. Ribbon windows incorporating a combination of fritted glass clerestories and louvered sunshades accomplish this goal. Spandrel alternatives include brick, metal panels, and glazed "shadow boxes."

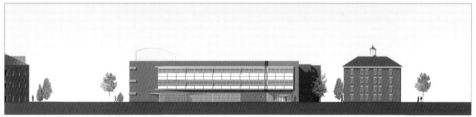

B2 Glass window with metal spandrel

Alt A – 6" Shelf   Alt B – 9" Shelf   Alt C – Two 6" Shelf   Alt D – 1' – 6" Sunscreen

 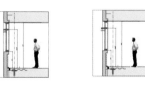 

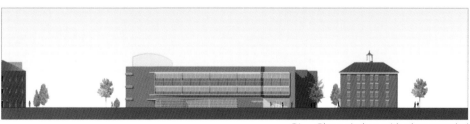

C1 Glass window with glass spandrel

June 21 12:00 PM June 21 12:00 PM June 21 12:00 PM June 21 12:00 PM

December 21 12:00 PM December 21 12:00 PM December 21 12:00 PM December 21 12:00 PM

C2 Glass window with shadow box

Existing	New renovation and addition

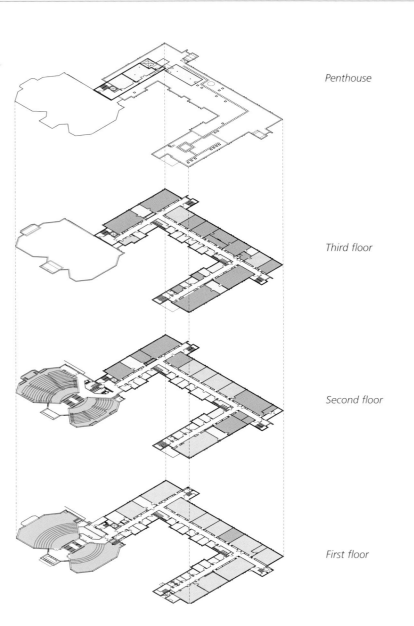
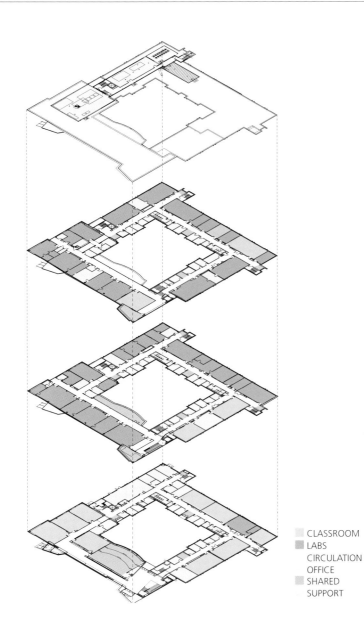

Penthouse

Third floor

Second floor

First floor

CLASSROOM
LABS
CIRCULATION
OFFICE
SHARED
SUPPORT

New Science Building Renovation and Addition

Connecting the legs of the existing building with the new addition eliminates dead-ends and provides continuous circulation on all floors of the building, significantly enhancing communication within and between the natural science departments. The addition's 14-foot floor-to-floor heights (compared with 12 feet for the existing building) accommodate new biology and chemistry teaching labs with their intensive fume hood and ventilation duct requirements. Negotiating the height differential between the new and the existing building is accomplished with short ramps at the east and west connection points. A new mechanical penthouse, with its fume-hood exhausts, is located on the west side of the building, maximizing its distance from a dormitory to the east. A shaft for the large fume-exhaust ducts is created by enclosing an exterior niche in the existing building. A major new duct shaft is introduced at the juncture of the new and existing building, optimizing its proximity to the areas with the greatest air supply and return requirements.

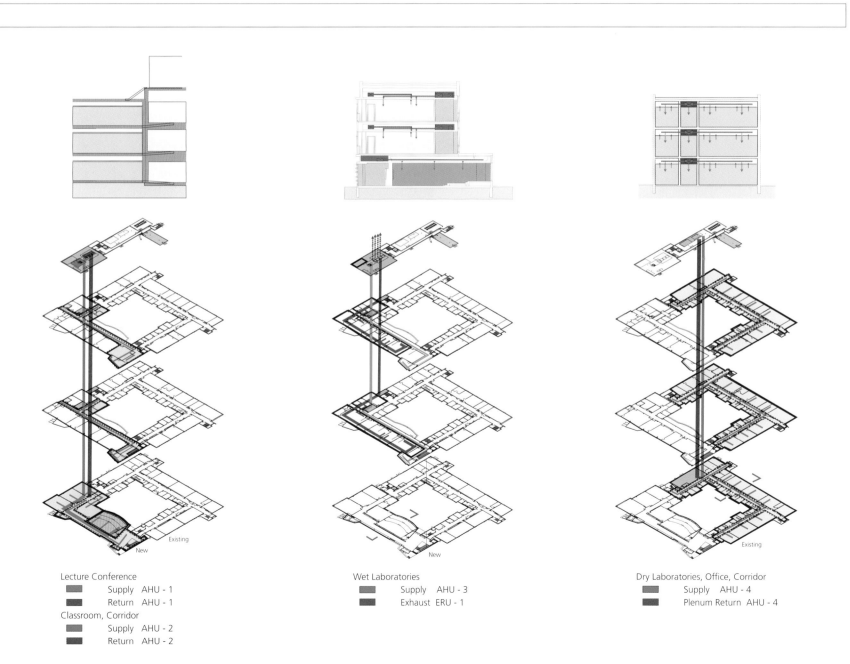

Lecture Conference
■ Supply   AHU - 1
■ Return   AHU - 1
Classroom, Corridor
■ Supply   AHU - 2
■ Return   AHU - 2

Wet Laboratories
■ Supply   AHU - 3
■ Exhaust ERU - 1

Dry Laboratories, Office, Corridor
■ Supply   AHU - 4
■ Plenum Return AHU - 4

"The *Windows into Science* are now complete along the Appian Way and they are just breathtaking from inside and outside. This morning I walked up Appian Way as a weather front rolled over Keene and I got to enjoy the reflections of the dramatic cloudscape, and reflections of campus scenery. The new windows let me look into the Science Center labs and out at the reflected world at the same time. The sun shelves reduce solar heat load under summer sun, while reflecting ambient light onto the ceilings of the labs. The overall effect is very 21st century, and the classic brickwork ties the building nicely to its surroundings."

Gordon Leversee, Dean of Sciences

Before

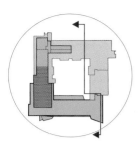

New addition wall section

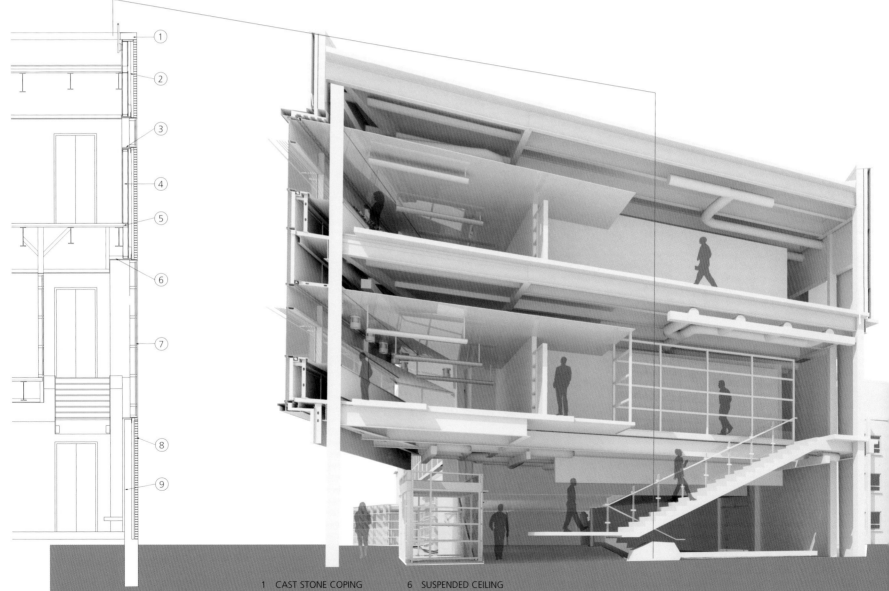

1	CAST STONE COPING	6	SUSPENDED CEILING
2	SPRAY FOAM INSULATION	7	ALUMINUM WINDOWS
3	SLATE STOOL	8	BRICK
4	STEEL STUDS @ 16" O.C.	9	CONCRETE BLOCK BACK-UP
5	CONCRETE FLOOR SLAB		

While the new addition is designed to accommodate the latest in teaching labs and large lecture rooms, the existing building is retrofitted with new HVAC, electric, and telecommunications systems to better serve the current and future needs of its faculty and students. Characteristic of most Boomer Buildings, the existing exterior had single-pane glazing and no insulation—a veritable energy sieve. This is rectified with a layer of 1 1/2-inch foil-faced polyisocayanurate rigid insulation applied to the in-board side of the existing CMU back-up wall. New high-performance low-e insulating glass units with warm-edge spacers replace the old windows.

| East stair | East wall | Existing wall section | Insulated wall section |

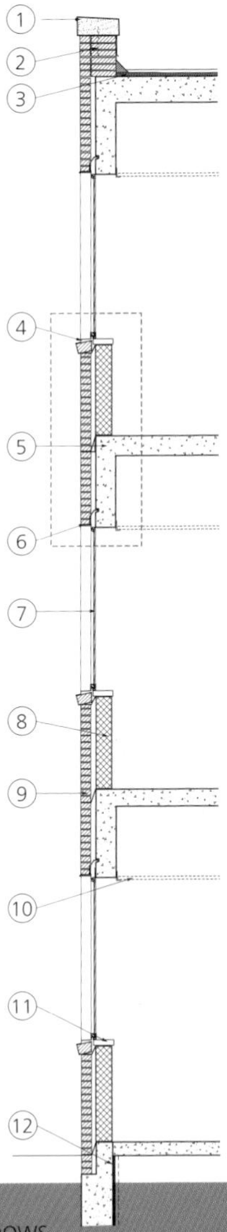

Insulated wall section labels:
SLATE STOOL
ALUMINUM SILL
ROWLOCK SILL
BRICK
CMU BACK-UP
RIGID INSULATION
METAL STUD WALL
GYPSUM WALL BOARD
FLASHING
WEEP HOLES
REGLET
LINTEL
SUSPENDED CEILING

Existing wall section numbered callouts: 1, 2, 3, 4, 5, 6, 7, 8, 9, 10, 11, 12

1	CAST STONE COPING	7	ALUMINUM WINDOWS
2	1/2" ZINC COATED ANCHORS	8	CMU BACK-UP
3	1 1/2" RIGID INSULATION	9	BRICK
4	ALUMINUM SILL	10	SUSPENDED CEILINGS
5	CONCRETE FLOOR SLAB	11	SLATE STOOL
6	LINTEL	12	1" ASPHALT RIGID INSULATION BOARD

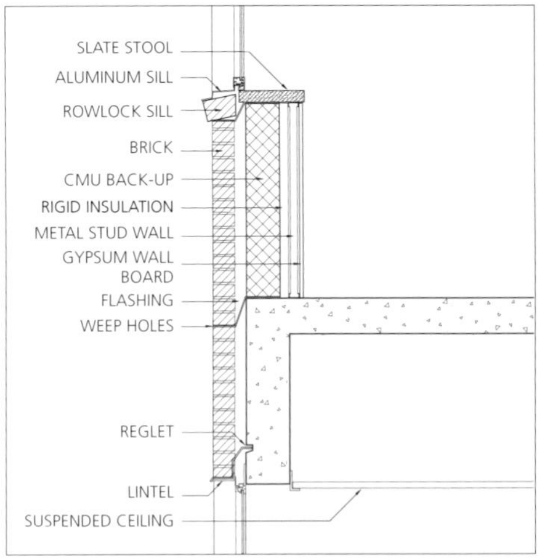

On the south elevation of the new addition, a high degree of energy efficiency is achieved through the use of solar shading devices, fritted glass clerestories, high-performance low-e insulating glass with warm-edge spacers, and shadow-box spandrels backed with spray-applied polyurethane foam insulation. The masonry portions of the addition consist of an air space behind which is polyurethane foam insulation spray-applied to gypsum sheathing and attached to 6-inch metal studs. In both cases the spray-applied insulation acts as a moisture and vapor barrier. Special attention is given to air-infiltration detailing.

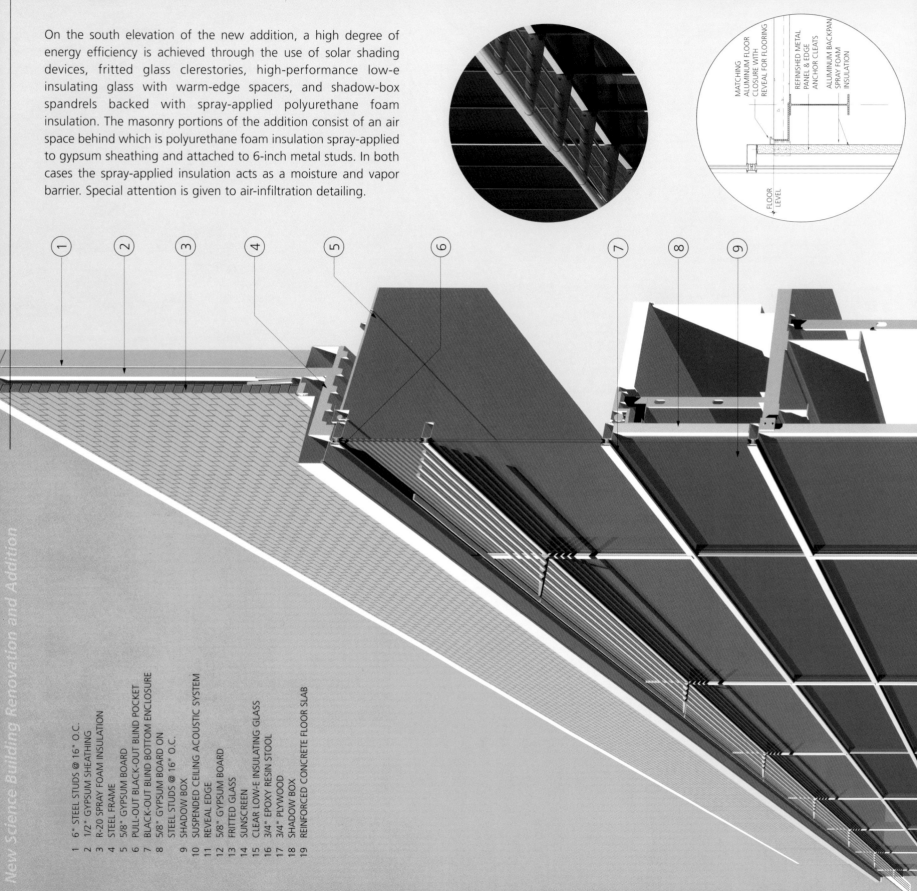

MATCHING ALUMINUM FLOOR CLOSURE WITH REVEAL FOR FLOORING

REFINISHED METAL PANEL & EDGE ANCHOR CLEATS

ALUMINUM BACKPAN SPRAY FOAM INSULATION

FLOOR LEVEL

New Science Building Renovation and Addition

1 6" STEEL STUDS @ 16" O.C.
2 1/2" GYPSUM SHEATHING
3 R-20 SPRAY FOAM INSULATION
4 STEEL FRAME
5 5/8" GYPSUM BOARD
6 PULL-OUT BLACK-OUT BLIND POCKET
7 BLACK-OUT BLIND BOTTOM ENCLOSURE
8 5/8" GYPSUM BOARD ON
   STEEL STUDS @ 16" O.C.
9 SHADOW BOX
10 SUSPENDED CEILING ACOUSTIC SYSTEM
11 REVEAL EDGE
12 5/8" GYPSUM BOARD
13 FRITTED GLASS
14 SUNSCREEN
15 CLEAR LOW-E INSULATING GLASS
16 3/4" EPOXY RESIN STOOL
17 3/4" PLYWOOD
18 SHADOW BOX
19 REINFORCED CONCRETE FLOOR SLAB

METAL FRAMING

6" METAL FRAMING

STEEL TEE SECTION & METAL DECK

METAL FRAMING

SPECIAL SHAPE MULLION CAP

ALUMINUM CLAD PANEL SYSTEM

MORTAR NET

SPRAY FOAM INSULATION

R-20

11

12

13

14

15

16

17

18

19

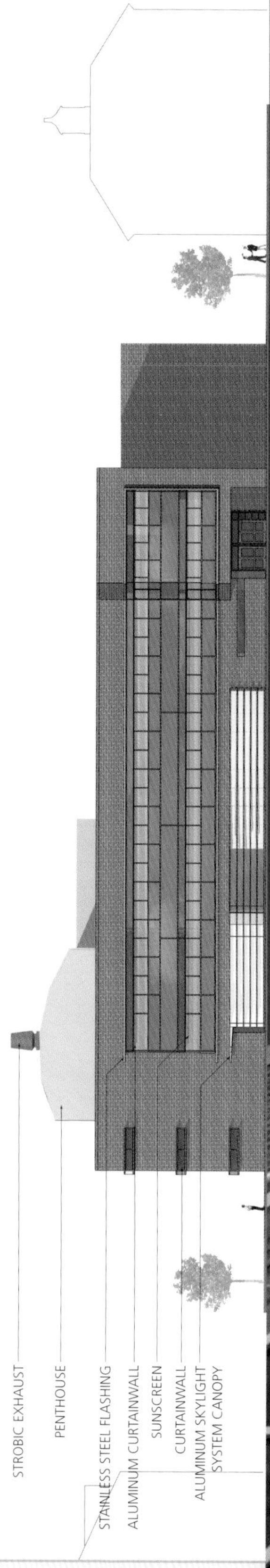

STROBIC EXHAUST

PENTHOUSE

STAINLESS STEEL FLASHING

ALUMINUM CURTAINWALL

SUNSCREEN

CURTAINWALL

ALUMINUM SKYLIGHT
SYSTEM CANOPY

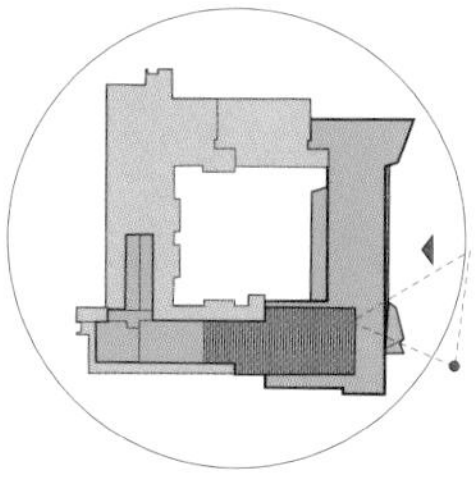

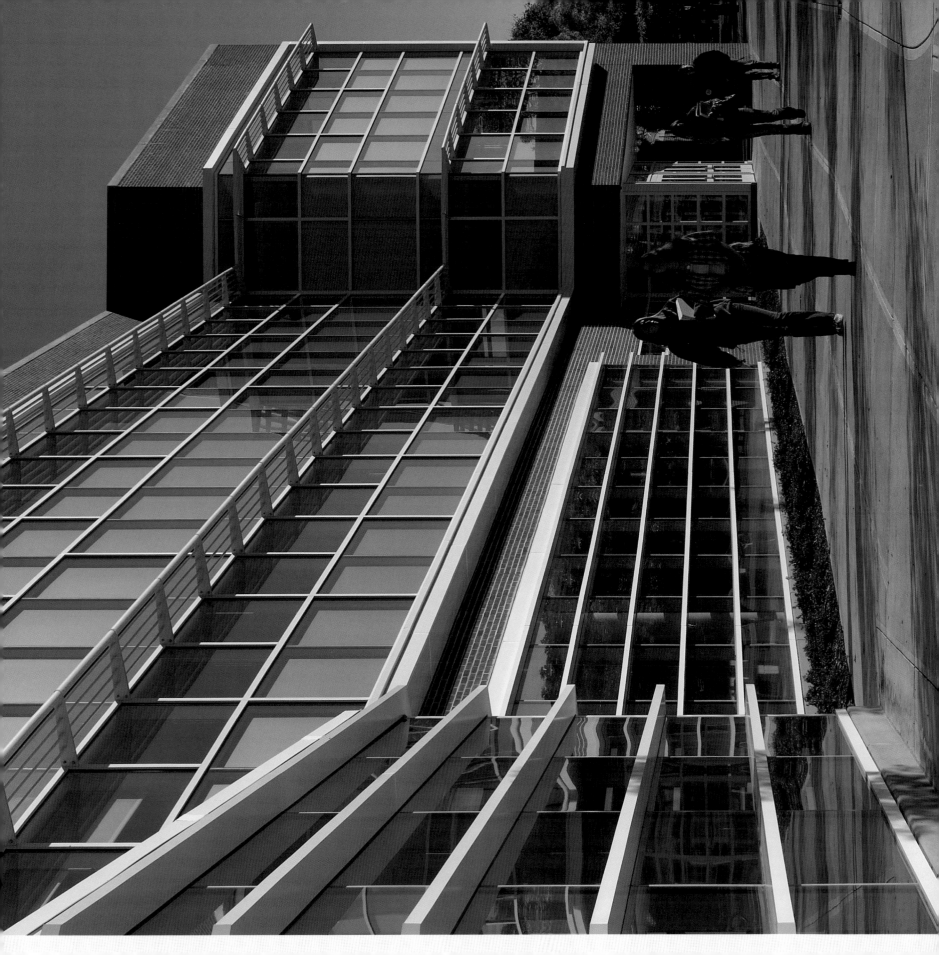

Courtyard (Before)

Typical of Boomer Buildings, the void between the legs of the Science Building was ill-defined, un-designed, "left over" space that no one used. It also introduced a gap in what was earlier intended as a New England urban esplanade. The expansion presented an opportunity to introduce positive open space in the heart of the project: a new science courtyard linked to the school's curriculum, with the bonus of a pleasant setting for casual gatherings. The design captures the essential character of the New Hampshire landscape, distilling it into an idealized snapshot of the region to help students learn about local botanical life and geological formations.

The Natural Science Department worked with the landscape architects, Dirtworks, Inc., to develop elements for use in teaching. The paving patterns and materials represent strata and native stone types. Large boulders suggest rock outcrops and provide opportunities to study natural rock formations. The plant palette is carefully selected to represent native New Hampshire flora as well as plants significant in botanical evolution.

Courtyard (Before)

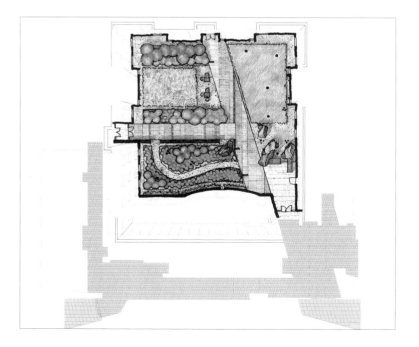

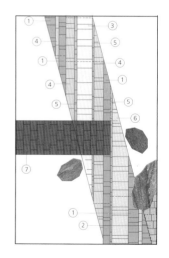

TYPE DESCRIPTION

1. BARRE GREY GRANITE
2. VERMONT GREEN SLATE
3. CAMBRIAN BLACK GRANITE
4. KERSHAW BEIGE GRANITE
5. WINNEWAY GRANITE
6. BLUESTONE
7. KIRBY LIMESTONE

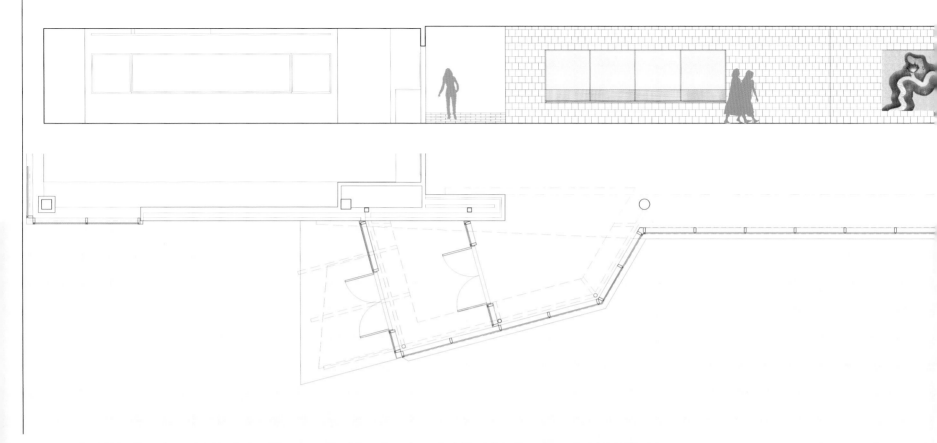

The new glazed entrance lobby fully engages life on the Appian Way and the Science Courtyard while providing access to the main lecture hall and large classrooms. Natural material finishes reflect the natural science programs: slate floors, ground-faced concrete masonry walls, maple benches and ceilings. The centerpiece of the lobby will be a specially commissioned 54-foot-long ceramic artwork by Nancy Selvage depicting a segment of the Ashuelot River as it would appear in a topographic map. The "water" will be of high-gloss glazed tile and will contain a variety of science-related images. The "banks" of the river will be substantial masses of unglazed ceramic, also containing scientific images embedded or impressed into the clay.

New Science Building Renovation and Addition

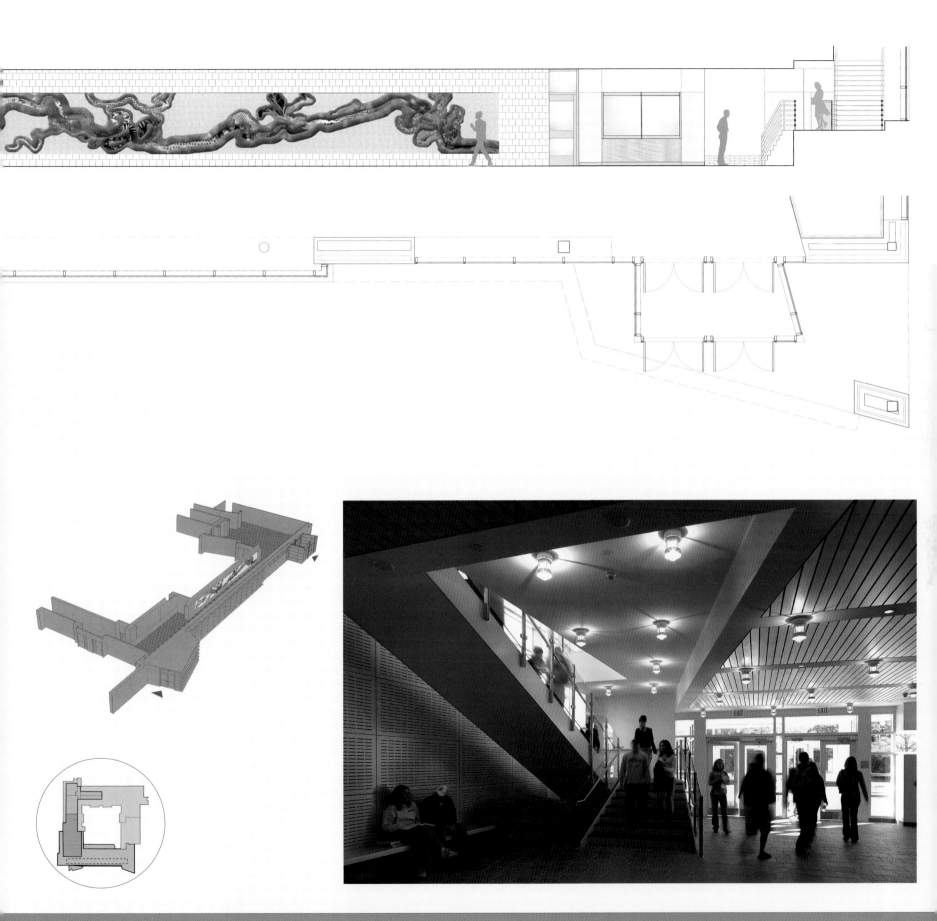

The new facility includes labs, classrooms, office, and support space that provide a functional, technically advanced environment to attract faculty and students to the programs housed in the Science Building. Entries, circulation, and public spaces in the new addition and renovated building are integrated with the new courtyard and Appian Way, enhancing the feeling of community and orientation for its occupants. The teaching and research labs accommodate the latest technology.

A consistent palette of materials and colors is used in both the existing building and the addition to reinforce the idea of a singular, unified building. Lab benches and storage cabinets are of maple veneer and epoxy-resin countertops. Additionally, the technological and systems upgrades in the existing building were equal to those of the addition. The lecture room casework features built-in power and data lines, permitting students to work together across the desks. It also has full audio-visual and distance-learning capability.

Abundant daylight pours into the labs through ribbon windows, in the galleries of the addition through floor-to-ceiling glass, and in the formerly windowless corridors of the existing building through "study nooks" that replace several offices.

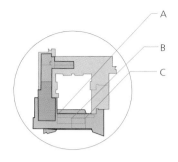

Lecture room (Before)

Lecture room (After)

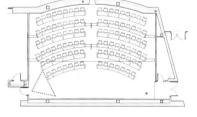

New Science Building Renovation and Addition

Corridor (Before)

North corridor

Lab (Before)

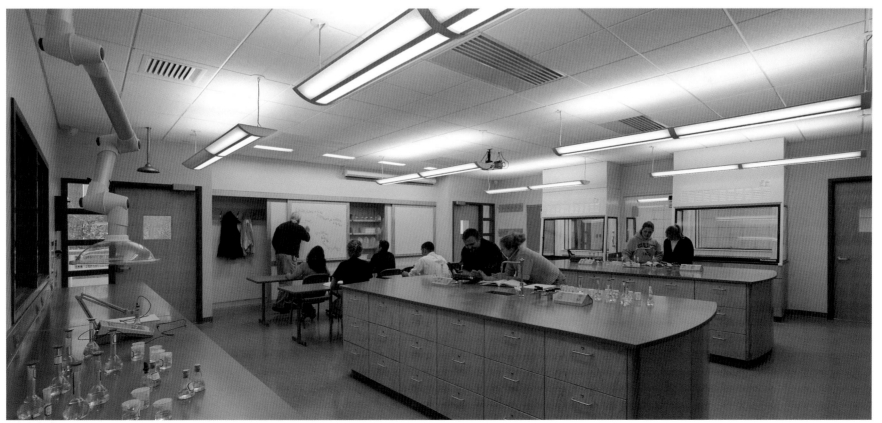

Lab (After)

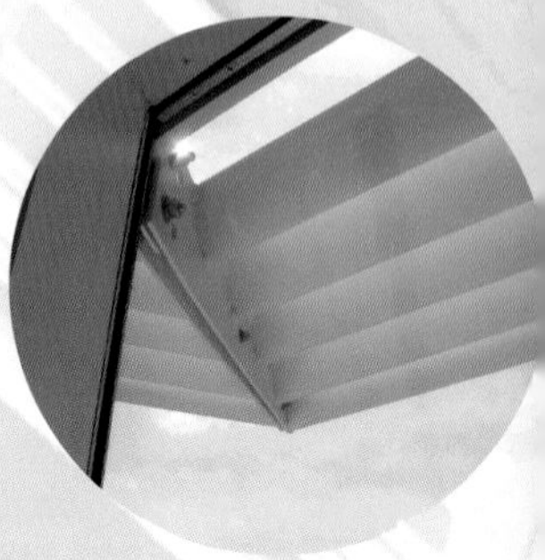

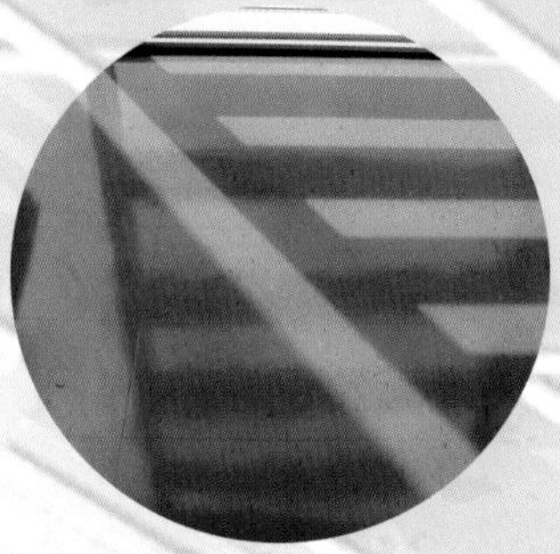

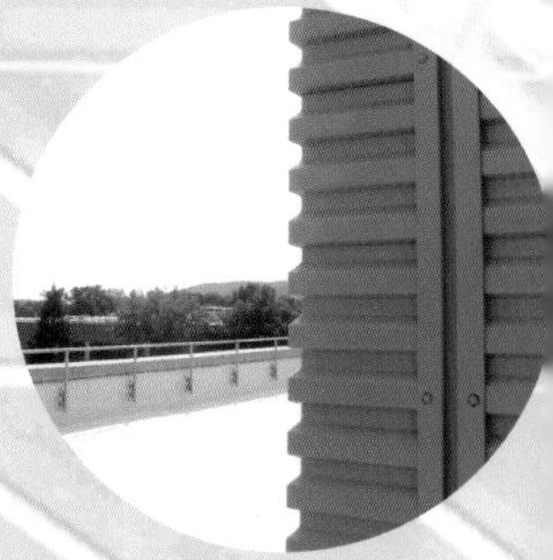

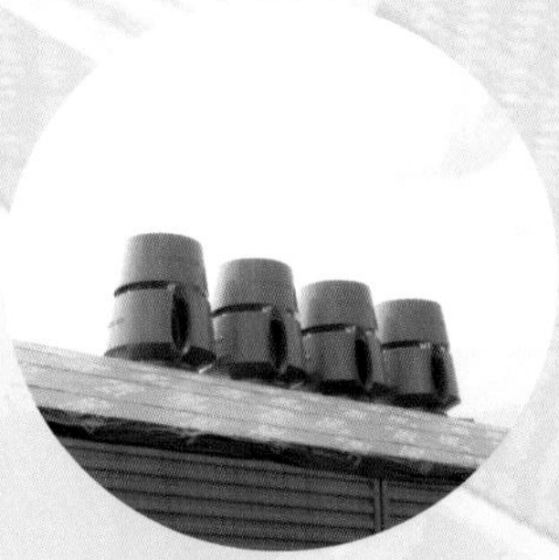

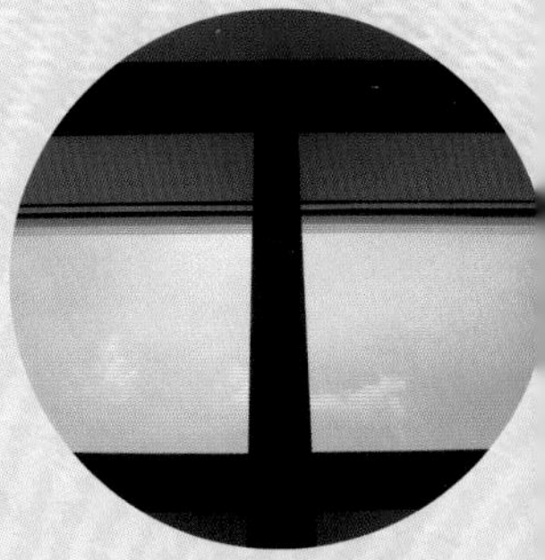

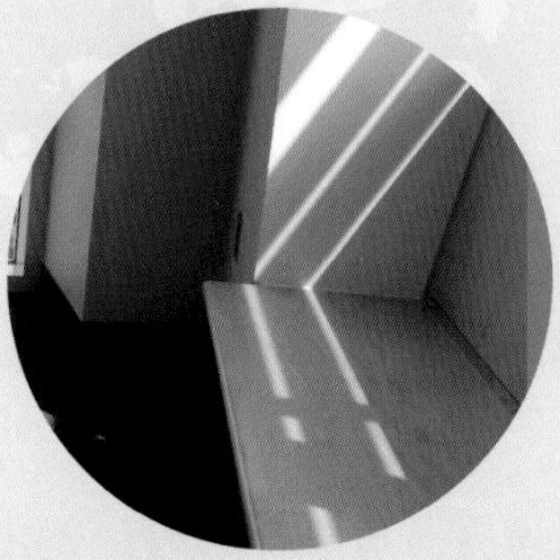

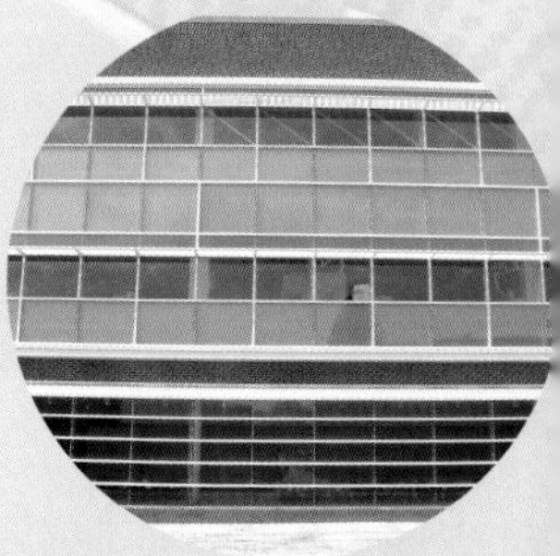

May 03
Occupant move out
Demolition of Lecture Hall
Construction Start – Renovation
Construction Start – Addition

Renovating and adding on to the Science Center instead of demolishing it and building anew resulted in a 93,640-square-foot facility constructed at a cost of $190 per square foot, compared to $250 per square foot for a new building. Such an approach also permitted an accelerated construction schedule—the Science Department reoccupied the building within one year.

06/16/2003   07/29/2003   10/06/2003   12/11/2003   01/13/2004

New Science Building Renovation and Addition

Classes start: August 04

Occupation move in: July 04

04/21/2004

04/29/2004
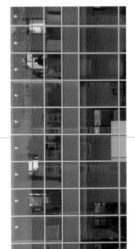
05/07/2004

05/18/2004

06/09/2004

Campus Intervention

- Elementary and High School, Spain

1991

1992

1993

1994

1995

1996
Master Plan

Construction
Phase I
1997

1998

1999

2000
Completion
Phase I

Construction
Phase II
2001

2002

2003

2004
Completion
Phase II E.S & Gym

Completion
Phase II H.S Gym
2005

Construction
Phase III
2006

During the 1950s a small residential community in southern Spain built a K–12 facility. Located on the coast, the 10 small classroom buildings comprising the campus were constructed of local materials, concrete, and stucco, and were sited to take advantage of the mild climate with exterior walkways and cross ventilation. Later buildings constructed in the 1960s were pre-fabricated steel structures, air conditioned with noisy roof-mounted HVAC units.

A 1996 assessment of the campus and its more than 20 buildings identified a wide range of deficiencies, both functional and physical. There was no clear separation or identification of the three school components: pre-school, elementary school, and high school. Confusing circulation patterns confounded pedestrians and motorists. Mechanical, electrical, and life safety systems were at the end of their useful lives. A surface stormwater system of open ditches severely limited the area available for playgrounds. In addition, buildings were in an advanced state of deterioration due to the effects of extreme drought cycles on the expansive soil conditions.

ELEMENTARY AND HIGH SCHOOL

Spain

☐ New Program
■ Updated Program
■ Updated Circulation
■ New MEP Telecom System
☐ Asbestos Removal
☐ New Exterior Wall
■ Addition
■ Renovation

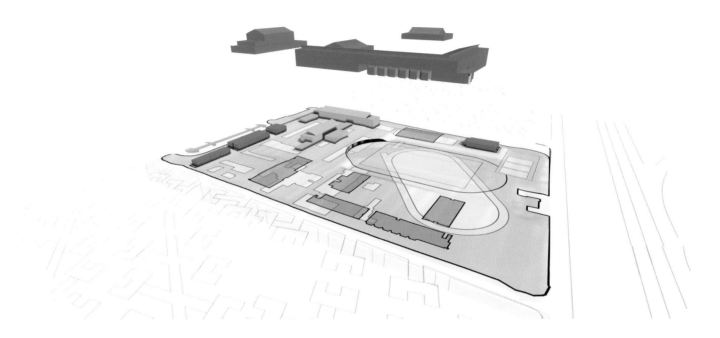

| *View 1* | *View 2* | *View 3* | *View 4* |

The campus is in the heart of a residential area. Students arrive by bus, automobile, bicycle, or on foot. The limited drop-off zone in the teacher parking area was very congested during arrival and departure periods with no marshalling area for students.

As the campus expanded from the original 10 buildings at the site's south end, the elementary facilities became disbursed along the west perimeter, resulting in a commingling of high school and elementary school facilities. The youngest students had the longest walk to the cafeteria, playgrounds, and main entrance.

The cafeteria/multipurpose room and the shared gym facility were located away from the school entrance on the east side of the site, removed from both the playgrounds and the ball field—not an ideal location.

A youth center on the campus was welcomed by families. However, its location adjacent to the school loading dock, remote from any playground, was a major program impediment.

Playgrounds, save for one, were located at the far corners of the site, so students crowded into one while the others lacked activity.

The dearth of a functional organization was reinforced by incoherent architectural expression. The utilitarian but consistent design of the early white stucco buildings gave way over time to an assemblage of random buildings in brick, industrial metal panels, and orange and tan stucco.

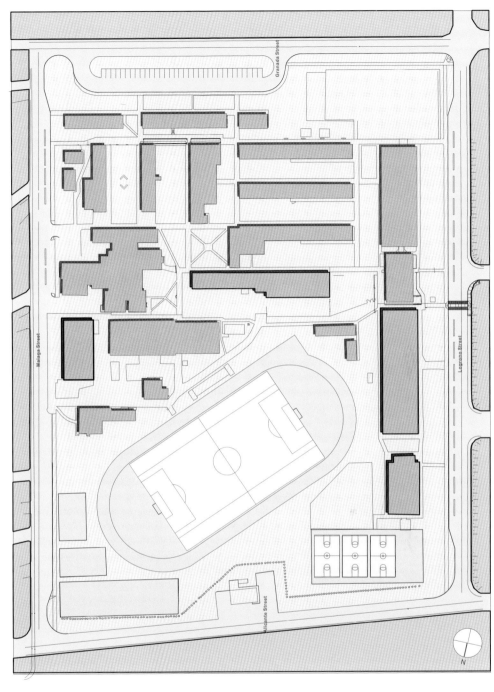

| *Program* | *Vehicular circulation* | *Pedestrian traffic* | *Public space* | *Utilities* |

Existing	*Phase I*	*Phase II*	*Phase III*	*Phase IV*

Preschool/Kindergarten
Elementary school
High school
Multipurpose
Youth Activity

To allow the schools to remain operational and to meet construction-funding cycles, a phased master plan for renovation and replacement of all campus facilities was developed. Rotating the central sport field to the west was key to creating usable building space.

The primary organizing element of the master plan is the creation of an identity for and consolidation of each school component. Three distinct bus/auto drop-off zones and entries are located on three sides of the campus. High school and elementary school arrival plazas with facilities for marshalling students and outdoor gatherings are located on the east and west sides of the campus adjacent to administration areas, gymnasiums, and the shared cafeteria/multipurpose room. The pre-school arrival area to the south facilitates its independent schedule and parental drop-off.

Design guidelines incorporating the regional architectural vocabulary of white stucco, glazed tile accents, pitched tile roofs, wooden doors, and shaded walkways were developed. A simplified plan of covered walks oriented to the center of the campus connects the new consolidated facilities.

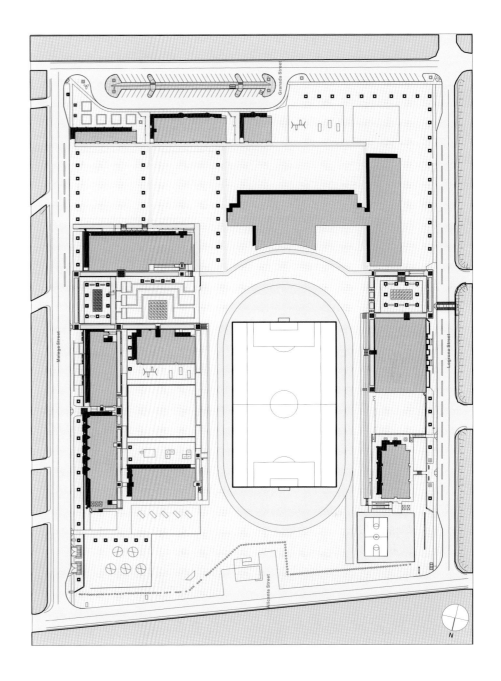

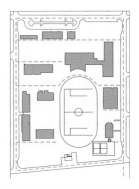

| *Vehicular circulation* | *Pedestrian traffic* | *Public space* | *Utilities* |

View A

The first phase began with construction of a new perimeter utility system and bus loading zones, followed by the renovation and expansion of the three classroom buildings to establish an identifiable pre-school entity on the south side of the campus. Significant foundation remediation was required to stabilize the structures. The perimeter utility system on the east and west sides of the campus was designed for incremental tie-ins from new east–west distribution systems under the campus walkways.

The Phase I covered walkway system was moved from the vehicular south side of these buildings to the north campus side where its sloped tile roof protects classroom entries. Operable windows allow cross ventilation in mild weather while perforated aluminum sunscreens admit light but block the direct sun.

Because the existing concrete structural frame and infill walls could not support the addition of sloped tile roofs, an independent structure was incorporated into the walkway design.

Plan and section (Before)

Plan and section (After)

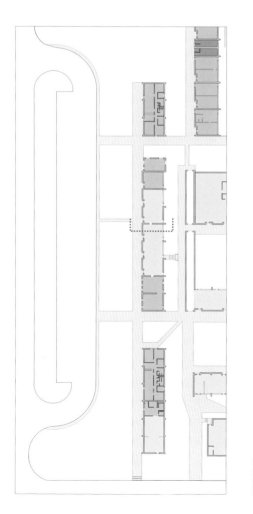

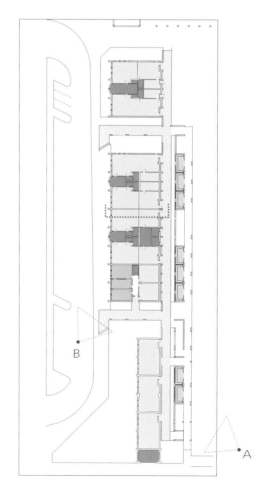

N

ADMIN./ GUIDANCE
MEDIA CENTER
GYM
MULTIPURPOSE
MEP/TOILETS/KITCHEN

View B

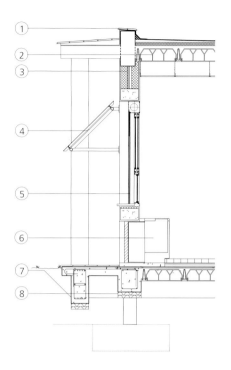

1 CLAY TILE COPING
2 PRECAST CONCRETE BEAMS
AND HOLLOW TILE FILLERS
3 STUCCO ON BLOCK
4 PERFORATED ALUMINUM
SUN SHADE
5 ALUMINUM WINDOW
WITH MARBLE SILL
6 HVAC UNIT
7 FOUNDATION PROTECTION
MEMBRANE
8 CORRUGATED CARDBOARD
FORM

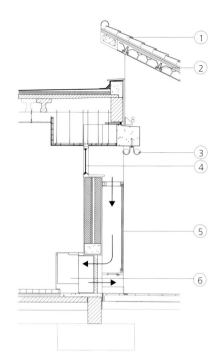

1 CLAY ROOF TILE
2 PRECAST CONCRETE BEAMS
AND HOLLOW TILE FILLERS
3 ACCESSIBLE COMMUNICATION
SYSTEMS CONDUITS
4 ALUMINUM WINDOW
WITH MARBLE SILL
5 DISPLAY CABINET
6 HVAC W/ SEPARATED SUPPLY
AND EXHAUST AIR

(Before)

(Before)

As proscribed by the design guidelines, white stucco walls, wood doors, and glazed tile accents unify the buildings. These mark classroom entries along with a "door mat" of paving tile and individual display cases. Some of the cabinets serve a double function in housing and separating the supply and exhaust louvers of the new HVAC units.

Solar shading along the south face prevents direct sunlight from entering the rooms, while the perforated surface creates dappled light in the upper window and on the shade's underside. Direct views are provided through the window's lower half. Special bay windows at each of the kindergarten kitchen/snack areas feature curved shades.

Along with stucco and tile finishes, local construction techniques were used. Structured concrete slabs are poured over a system of precast beams with leave-in-place infill clay tile formwork. The cast-in-place concrete support beams are isolated from expansive soil effects with the use of special corrugated cardboard formwork.

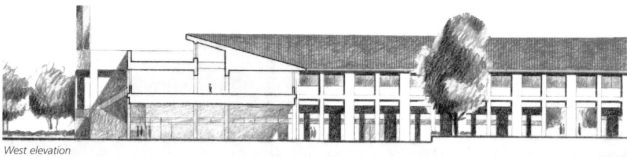

West elevation

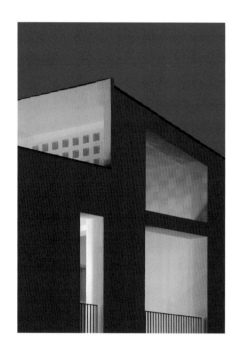

1 TILE ROOF
2 PRECAST CONCRETE BEAMS
    AND HOLLOW TILE FILLERS
3 CONCRETE BEAM
4 ACOUSTICAL CEILING
5 PERFORATED ALUMINUM
    SUN SHADE
6 ALUMINUM WINDOW
    W/MARBLE SILL
8 STUCCO CEILING
9 CONCRETE WALL
10 CORRUGATED CARDBOARD
    FORMWORK

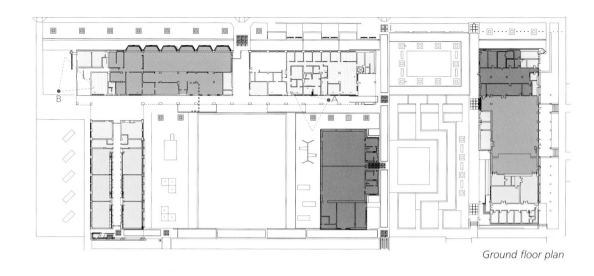

Ground floor plan

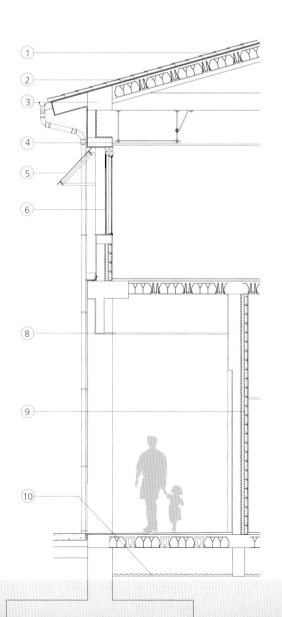

View A

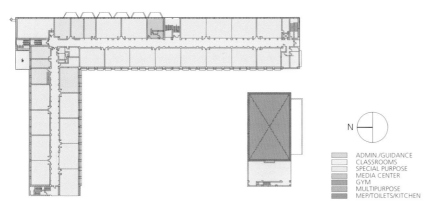

N

ADMIN./GUIDANCE
CLASSROOMS
SPECIAL PURPOSE
MEDIA CENTER
GYM
MULTIPURPOSE
MEP/TOILETS/KITCHEN

First floor plan

Consolidating the elementary school and high school into separate two-story buildings creates two distinct educational entities and provides the opportunity to significantly increase the outdoor play areas and separate them by age group. Ground-floor arcades and open stairs continue the walkway system while the sloped tile roofs create a second floor corridor similar to the Phase I covered walkway.

Geography strongly influenced the design of all phases of the school. Southern Spain enjoys the strong contrasts of sun and shade. Far west in its time zone, it is the late sunrise rather than the early sunset that defines winter. These unique characteristics are emphasized in the play of shadows and indirect light in the walkways, and the morning glow through the screened walls of the stairs.

The U-shaped plan creates a focus on central gathering and play areas, reinforced by the slope of the clay tile roofs. Continued adherence to the design guidelines, including stucco walls in an articulated structural frame and perforated aluminum sunshades, ties the new large-scale construction with the smaller Phase I renovation, creating a unified image. Administration offices, classrooms, the media center, and the gymnasium are the core elements of the new elementary school.

View B

View C

East elevation

As with the special buildings in the surrounding Andalusian towns, decorative glazed tile highlights entries and creates accents. Entry portals with blue tile grids signal both the elementary and high school arrival plazas and their adjacent administrative offices. From the surrounding area, tile-topped chimneys distinguish the school complex as the community's heart. The media center is articulated with special round-tile-trimmed windows.

The construction of the elementary school continues to incorporate the local precast and tile infill slab and formwork system. Isolation from the expansive soils is achieved with heavily loaded, deep footings and use of the corrugated cardboard formwork under the intermediate beams.

A drought-resistant, low maintenance landscape palette included in the design guidelines was used in both the first and second phases of construction. Between the sidewalk of the three drop-off zones and the buildings, a surface of compacted stone dust accommodates bike racks, trees, and defined areas with low flowering shrubs such as lantana. Palm trees, some new and some relocated, define major walkways and entries. Shade trees are found at the perimeter of play areas. The campus drops 12 feet from south to north, requiring a series of ramps and berms planted with local ground cover. Mowed Bermuda grass is limited to the ball fields and a special gathering area at the center of the elementary school. The play areas are finished in terra cotta colored asphalt.

View A

Elementary and High School

View B

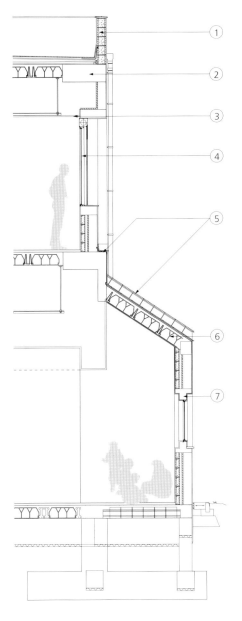

1 CONCRETE BLOCK PARAPET
2 CONCRETE BEAM
3 ACOUSTICAL CEILING
4 ALUMINUM WINDOW
  W/MARBLE SILL
5 BASETILE AND CATALAN TILE
6 PRECAST CONCRETE BEAMS
  AND HOLLOW TILE FILLERS
7 CONCRETE LINTEL

Media center

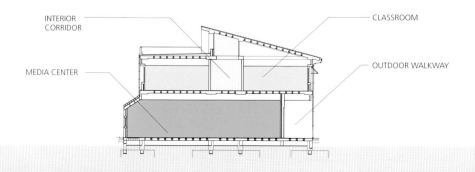

INTERIOR CORRIDOR

CLASSROOM

MEDIA CENTER

OUTDOOR WALKWAY

Classroom

As part of the elementary school's arrival sequence the media center's bay windows with their tile trim are a welcoming expression of the school's collective experience. On the interior they provide gathering areas for quiet work as well as group discussion. In addition to computer areas for work and research the media center has a separate glass-enclosed computer instruction room.

The Phase I vocabulary of wood doors and tile sign panels is extended to the elementary school classrooms. Corridor floors include terra cotta tile in geometric patterns similar to those found in the surrounding region. The clerestory provides indirect light to the second floor corridor while the articulated structure creates recesses for lockers and display boards, giving the elementary school's corridor and covered walkway of the pre-school a common expression.

Classrooms are designed to accommodate the varying teaching requirements of first through sixth grade. Adjustable height white boards, a wall of cork-covered storage cabinets, a continuous expanse of operable glazing, and individual room HVAC controls create an environment easily adapted to teacher and class needs.

Corridor

In addition to the elementary school, Phase II includes the high school gymnasium, a sports field, outdoor basketball facilities, and a youth center, which complete the redevelopment of the northern half of the campus. Phases III and IV, the multipurpose room and high school in the center section of the campus will complete the full school renovation and reconstruction.

An early economic analysis showed that renovation and expansion of the Phase I buildings would provide swing space to facilitate the phased replacement of the remainder of the school facilities. Due to the destructive soil conditions and the inefficient building sizes, it was less costly to replace and consolidate the majority of the buildings than to renovate them. However, the regional strengths of the original buildings—white stucco to reflect the sun, covered walkways, and concrete frame and infill structure—became the unifying design vocabulary for the full campus.

Appendix

- Historical Notes/Credits

- Boomer Building Experience

- Firm Profile

- Acknowledgments

The Lighthouse International Headquarters
The Lighthouse Inc.
New York, New York

ORIGINAL BUILDING
Architect: Kahn & Jacobs
Year completed: 1964

Building use: The Lighthouse Manhattan Headquarters. (Since 1906, The Lighthouse has assisted the visually impaired population through direct services and professional and public education programs.)

RENOVATION/ADDITION

Owner: The Lighthouse Inc.

Architect: Mitchell | Giurgola Architects

Construction manager: Barr & Barr, Inc.
MEP: Cosentini Associates
Structural: Severud Associates
Lighting: H.M. Brandston & Partners, Inc.
Graphics and wayfinding: Whitehouse & Company

Powdermaker Hall
Queens College, The City University of New York
Flushing, New York

ORIGINAL BUILDING
Architect: DeYoung, Moskowitz and Rosenburg
Year completed: 1962

Building use: Main classroom building at Queens College

RENOVATION

Owner: Dormitory Authority of the State of New York

Architect: Mitchell | Giurgola Architects

Construction manager: E&F/Walsh Building Company, LLC
MEP: Mariano D. Molina P.C.
Site civil: Langan Engineering and Environmental Services
Structural: Ysrael A. Seinuk, P.C.
Landscape architect: Thomas Balsley Associates
Specifications: Robert Schwartz & Associates
Lighting designer: Brandston Partnership Inc.
Cost consultant: Wolf and Company
Acoustical: Shen Milsom & Wilke, Inc.
Vertical/Elevator: Van Deusen Associates
Higher education program and planning consultant: Scott Blackwell Page, AIA

New York County Family Court
Dormitory Authority of the State of New York
New York, New York

ORIGINAL BUILDING
Architect: Haines, Lundberg & Waehler (HLW)
Year completed: 1975

Building use: Family Court

RENOVATION

Owner: Dormitory Authority of the State of New York; Office of Court Administration, New York State

Architect: Mitchell | Giurgola Architects

Construction manager: E&F /Walsh Building Company, LLC
Court planning: Richard Halpert
MEP: Cosentini Associates
Structural: Ysrael A. Seinuk
Curtainwall: R.A. Heintges Consultants
Geotech/Site/Civil: Langan Engineering and Environmental services
Cost consultant: Wolf and Company
Lighting consultant: Cline Bettridge Bernstein Lighting design
Security: Kroll Inc.
Acoustical: Cerami & Associates, Inc
Signage: Calori & Vanden-Eynden
Code: Municipal Expediting, Inc.
Specifications: Robert Schwartz & Associates

Boyd Science Hall
Plymouth State University
Plymouth, New Hampshire

ORIGINAL BUILDING

Architect: Alonzo J. Harriman Associates, Inc.,
Architect-Engineers, Auburn, Maine
Year completed: 1969

Building use: 57,191-square-foot three-story
brick and precast concrete multipurpose facility
(classroom and lab building for Natural Sciences
Dept.)

RENOVATION/ADDITION

Owner: Plymouth State University
University System of New Hampshire

Design architect: Mitchell | Giurgola Architects

Architect of record: Banwell Architects, Inc.

General contractor: Harvey Construction
Corporation
MEP, Structural, Site/Civil: Rist-Frost Shumway
Engineering, PC
Landscape architect: G2 + 1, LLC
Lighting: Brandston Partnership, Inc.

New Science Building
Keene State College
Keene, New Hampshire

ORIGINAL BUILDING

Architect: Frank Grad & Sons, Newark, NJ
Year completed: 1967

Building use: Science center, with a small
addition in 1984

RENOVATION/ADDITION

Owner: Keene State College
University System of New Hampshire

Design architect: Mitchell | Giurgola Architects

Architect of record: Banwell Architects, Inc.

Construction manager/General contractor:
Gilbane Building Company
MEP: Rist-Frost Shumway Engineering
Civil: Clough, Harbour & Associates
Structural: McFarland-Johnson Inc.
Courtyard landscape architect: Dirtworks, Inc.
Landscape architect: Vanessa Hangen Brustlin, Inc.
Cost estimator: Hanscomb USA
Lighting designer: Brandston Partnership Inc.

Elementary and High School
Spain

ORIGINAL BUILDING

Architect: Unknown
Year completed: 1954, 1958

Building use: The 1954 building was a single
room located in a field near a tiny Spanish
fishing village, with 28 students from K–12.
School buildings and facilities in the present
housing area began in September 1958, when
enrollment grew to 1300 students in K–6 and
750 in 7–12. After 1978 enrollment dropped.
Currently 600 in K–6 and 270 in 7–12.

MASTER PLAN/ADDITIONS

Architect: Mitchell | Giurgola Architects

Associate architect: G y A Promotories, S.L.

MEP: Flack + Kurtz; G y A Promotories, S.L.
Site/Civil: Langan; G y A Promotories, S.L.
Structural: Weidlinger Associate; G y A
Promotories, S.L.
Landscape architect: Rolland/Towers, LLC
Cost consultant: Hanscomb Associates

Before   After

Student Union, State University College at Plattsburgh
New York State University Construction Fund
Plattsburgh, New York
Completion: 1974

Benjamin F. Feinberg Library, State University College at Plattsburgh
New York State University Construction Fund
Plattsburgh, New York
Completion: 1977

Sherman Fairchild Center for Life Sciences
Columbia University
New York, New York
Completion: 1979
Original: 1960's building

Anchorage Museum of Art and History
City of Anchorage
Anchorage, Alaska
Completion: 1986
Original: 1960's building

Office Renovation, 1 Chase Manhattan Plaza
The Chase Manhattan Bank, N.A.
New York, New York
Completion: 1990
Original: 1960

Casa Manana Theatre, Renovation and Expansion
City of Fort Worth
Fort Worth, Texas
Project: 1991
Original: 1960's building

The Lighthouse International Headquarters
The Lighthouse Inc.
New York, New York
Completion: 1994
Original: 1960's building

Access Project
Community Church of New York
New York, New York
Completion: 1995
Original: 1940's building

Courtyard and Lobby Renovation
New School University
New York, New York
Completion: 1997
Original: 1959

New Gymnasium, Columbus East High School
Bartholomew Consolidated School Corporation
Columbus, Indiana
New Gymnasium Completion: 1999
Original: 1970's building

Elementary and High School

Completion: 1999

Original: 1950's and 1960's buildings

Teaching and Learning Center

New York University School of Medicine

New York, New York

Completion: 1998

Original: 1960's building

Weiss Building Renovations

Population Council

New York, New York

Completion: 2001

Original: 1960's building

Administration and Student Services Building Renovation

Hostos Community College

The City University of New York

Bronx, New York

Completion: 2002

Original: 1960's building

Master Plan

New Brunswick Theological Seminary

New Brunswick, New Jersey

Completion: 2006

Original: 1960's master plan

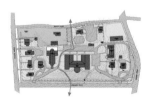

Boyd Hall Renovation and Addition

Plymouth State University

Plymouth, New Hampshire

Completion: 2003

Original: 1960's building

Powdermaker Hall Renovation

Queens College, The City University of New York

Queens, New York

Completion: 2004

Original: 1962

New Science Building
Keene State College

Lebanon, New Hampshire

Completion: 2004

Original: 1960's

Tilles Performing Arts Center Renovation
and Reconstruction

Long Island University, C.W. Post Campus

Brookville, New York

Completion: 2005

Original: 1981

New York County Family Court Renovation

New York, New York

Completion: 2005

Original: 1960's building

Three Rivers Community College

Norwich, Connecticut

Completion: 2008

Original: 1950's and 1960's building

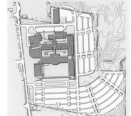

The case studies presented herein reflect Mitchell | Giurgola's continuing tradition of architecture in which the buildings created represent a synthesis of architectural mass, craft and their natural surrounding. Since its founding in 1958, the firm has dedicated itself to the creation of a sustainable architecture that has the ability to repair dysfunctional buildings and urban settings, set the groundwork for sensible patterns to restructure communities, and introduce new and renovated structures that will enhance our daily routines.

The success of the firm is measured by its long-standing ability to successfully serve its clients by maintaining a program-derived and site-sensitive approach to design. Mitchell | Giurgola is proud of the recognition it has been awarded through continuous publication of its work, successful entries in design competitions as well as the receipt of more that 75 professional honor awards for completed projects.

The six projects presented in this volume were led by the firm's partners: James Braddock, Paul Broches, Steven Goldberg, Jan Keane, John Kurtz and Carol Loewenson. The partners bring diverse perspectives to their work and through frequent on-the-boards deliberations and peer review, a vision for each project emerges which contributes to the shared vision and collaborative environment fostered by the close-knit studio setting at Mitchell | Giurgola.

The partners do not favor the imposition any particular style on their work. The form of a given project evolves in direct response to the program and its specific site characteristics. Ultimately, each building emerges from its context to take on a presence and definition that is unique. It is the tension between these seemingly contradictory qualities that defines the work of Mitchell | Giurgola. The firm's designs are a result of a unique architectural expression informed by history, culture and human behavior.

Mitchell | Giurgola Architects remains committed to a humanist practice of architecture dedicated to the belief that architecture is capable of enriching the daily experience. The firm continues to build responsibly and with integrity while striving to create a sense of the whole through designs that relate to and integrate interiors with exteriors and structures with landscapes.

Mitchell | Giurgola Architects

Partners – James Braddock; Paul Broches; Steven Goldberg; Jan Keane; John Kurtz; Carol Loewenson; **Associate Partner** – Susan Stando; **Associates** – Stephen Dietz; John Doherty **Staff** – Tony Alfieri; Jason Balecha; Tom Beck; Aliki Boudounis; Faek Braick; Russ Crader; Delphine Daniels; Rosa Dunn; David Evans; Carl Gruswitz; You-Chang Jeon; Carrie Johnson; Joshua Ledesma;Jennifer Lee; Sangwoo Lee; Wai-Yin Leung; Melida Marte; Mariella Mayrina; Michelle Parkinson; John Phillips; Heidi Sadler; Temitayo Shajuyigbe; Jillian Sheedy; Tyson Siegele; Yu-Lin Wang; Beverly Welch

The Partners: Steven Goldberg (FAIA), Carol Loewenson (AIA), Paul Broches (FAIA), Jan Keane (FAIA), John Kurtz (AIA), and James Braddock (AIA). At Lighthouse International Headquarters. Artwork: Sol LeWitt

ACKNOWLEDGMENTS

Contributors to Introduction:
Lia Gartner
Steven Goldberg
Jan Keane
Christa Mahar
Mildred Schmertz
Alan Traugott

Book and graphic design:
You-Chang Jeon

Graphic illustration:
You-Chang Jeon
Elizabeth Engler
Jennifer Lee
Jason Balecha

Photography:
Mitchell | Giurgola Architects,
except as noted below:

Jeff Goldberg/ESTO:
12, 18–19, 20 (After), 20 (Upper
right), 20 (Upper left), 21 (After),
22 (After), 23, 24 (After), 25 (View
1, 2), 26, 27, 28 (After), 29,
32–33, 38, 43 (After), 45 (Lower
right), 47, 48 (After), 49 (After),
50 (View A, B, C), 51 (View E, G,
H), 52 (After), 53 (Right), 67, 68,
69, 80, 89, 90 (Left), 91 (Top), 92,
93 (Upper right), 94, 95, 96, 97
(View B, C), 99, 100 (Bottom), 101
(Upper right), 103 (Center), 113,
115 (East Wall), 116, 118, 119,
121 (Bottom), 122, 123, 124
(Bottom), 125 (North Corridor,
Bottom), 129 (Top), 138, 139
(Bottom), 140 (Lower right), 142
(Upper left, Bottom), 143
(Bottom), 145, 146 (View A, C),
147, 148, 149, 156 (Office
Renovation After), 157
(Community Church of New York
After), 158 (Teaching and Learning
Center After), 158 (Boyd Hall
After), 159 (Keene State College
After).

Jeff Goldberg/Composited by
Mitchell | Giurgola Architects:
56, 63, 67.

Bernstein Associates:
30–31 (Thumbnails).

Dirtworks, Inc.:
120 (Upper Left), 121 (All except
bottom), 128–129 (Bottom
thumbnails).

Keene State College:
128 (Upper and lower right black
and white).

The Lighthouse, Inc:
15 (Old), 18 (Old), 24 (Before), 25
(Before), 28 (Before).

Jack Pottle:
6–17 (Models), 85 (Models), 156
(Sherman Fairchild Center for Life
Science After), 157 (Casa Manana
After).

Queens College:
34 (View D), 35.

Plymouth State University:
102–103 (Bottom and top
thumbnails).

John Veltri:
156 (Student union).

George Cserma:
156 (SUNY Plattsburgh Benjamin
F. Feinberg Library).

Paul Warchol:
156 (Anchorage Museum of Art
and History After).

Michael Van Valkenburgh
Associates:
157 (New School University
Before).

Chuck Choi:
157 (New School University After).

Morgan Construction Enterprises:
158 (Weiss Building Renovation
After).

Norman McGrath:
159 (Tilles Performing Arts Center
Renovation and Reconstruction
Exterior Before, Interior After).